This book is due for return on or before the last date shown below.

Dandies

PAGEANT OF HISTORY   EDITOR: JOHN GROSS

James Laver

Dandies

WEIDENFELD AND NICOLSON 5 WINSLEY STREET LONDON WI

SBN 297 76388 1
Designed by Hewat/Swift/Walters Limited
for George Weidenfeld and Nicolson Limited, London

Printed in Great Britain by Ebenezer Baylis & Son, Limited
The Trinity Press, Worcester, and London

'Dandyism appears especially in the
transitory periods when democracy is not yet
all-powerful, and when aristocracy is only
partially unsettled and depreciated . . .
Dandyism is the last splendour of heroism
in decadence . . . Dandyism is a setting sun;
like the star in its decline, it is superb,
without heat and full of melancholy.'

CHARLES BAUDELAIRE

Contents

1
Dandyism and George Brummell

Fine feathers make fine birds; but it is obvious even to the most unobservant that the fine bird in question is almost invariably the male. It is he who sports the crest and spreads the peacock tail; it is he whose neck gleams with the iris of iridescent feathers when his poor wife is nothing but a drab and humdrum fowl. So the rule would seem to run through the whole animal creation; and for the greater part of history it has been the same with the human male.

We have only to call up in imagination almost any figure from the past to see that this is true. We watch Henry VIII of England and Francis I of France meeting on what is still called the Field of the Cloth of Gold. Sir Walter Raleigh wore a fortune on his back; and, in the next generation, the first Duke of Buckingham is reported to have worn a suit of white velvet embellished with precious stones to the value of seventy thousand pounds. The courtiers of Charles II, like those of his contemporary Louis XIV, dripped with costly lace. The coat of the early eighteenth-century 'beau' was even more elaborately embroidered than his lady's gown. Two generations later the 'macaroni' employed every device of elaborate ostentation. Then, in a little more than a decade, half way through the reign of George III, it all stopped. Men made what has been called 'the great renunciation'; and they have been pretty drab ever since.

Beaux, macaronis and dandies are sometimes spoken of (even in serious works of costume history) as if they fell into the same category. In reality they are sharply divided: the beaux and macaronis on one side and the dandies on the other. We shall never understand dandyism unless we realize that whatever else it was it was the *repudiation* of fine feathers. What then *is* dandyism, and how did it come about?

Clothes are never a frivolity. They are always an expression of the fundamental social and economic pressures of the time. In his study *The Economics of Fashion* the economist Paul H. Nystrom states that 'in a sense, the development of this movement of dandyism, if it may be so termed, rose during the eighteenth and nineteenth centuries as a protest against the rule of kings in the field of fashion, as democracy rose as a protest against the rule of kings in politics.' This is undoubtedly true even if we have to make a few reservations about the use of the word democracy in this connection. The protest was certainly against the rule of kings, but it is only by a straining of language that we can call the protesters democrats.

It is no accident that the process began in England. After the 'Glorious Revolution' of 1689 the Court ceased to be the centre of social life. It had been the deliberate policy of Louis XIV to make the French aristocracy dance attendance on him at Versailles, in a word, to turn them all into courtiers. Courtiers they remained until the French Revolution and they wore the clothes appropriate to a Court: embroidered coats, white silk stockings, lace at wrist and throat, *talons rouges*, powdered hair. But in England the situation was quite different. The men who had made the Revolution of 1689, the great landed proprietors and their lesser brethren, the minor nobility and the 'country gentlemen' (revealing name) did not spend their time fluttering round a Court; they spent it on their estates.

Their pursuits were 'country' pursuits, chiefly, of course, fox hunting. And it soon became obvious to them that the clothes of the French courtier were quite unsuitable for so strenuous a pastime. They therefore simplified their dress. For an embroidered coat they substituted one of plain cloth, and they cut away the skirts at the front in order that they might sit on a horse more easily. Instead of lace ruffles at the wrist they wore plain linen, instead of the lace *rabat* they wore a neckcloth and

From *Le Jardin de la Noblesse Française*, by Adrian Bosse, 1629

instead of white silk stockings and buckled shoes, stout riding boots. They found that the three-cornered hat was too wide in the brim and too low in the crown (it was easily blown off and did not save your head when you fell on it) and so they shrank the brim almost to nothing and raised the crown, thereby creating a primitive crash-helmet – and the first top hat. All this happened about 1760; and what we have been describing is, with slight modifications, the dress of the dandy of half a century later.

Perhaps the real turning point was when the famous Coke of Norfolk, one of the richest and most enlightened landowners of his time, came to London to present a petition to George III. He did so in the country clothes he wore every day, that is, in riding clothes, in 'sports costume'. This was indeed a portent of the shape of things to come.

Such a thing could only have happened in England and, indeed, it might not have influenced anywhere else but for that revolt of the *grande bourgeoisie* which is known to the history books as the French Revolution. The men who made it had long seen on the other side of the Channel much that appealed to their new craving for liberty. They saw in the English country gentleman something approaching their ideal of the free and happy man. Admiration promotes imitation and so, when the Terror had subsided (and during the Terror it was unwise to wear fine clothes of any kind), English country clothes began to be worn in Paris. It is true that the young Incroyables of the Directoire period wore them in an exaggerated and even fantastic form, but the intention was plain enough.

With such exaggeration the English dandies would have nothing to do, and the man who set himself most firmly against anything of the kind was the Prince of the Dandies, Brummell himself; and where Brummell led others followed. But how did he ever attain – and retain – a pre-eminence universally acknowledged in his own lifetime and since?

He started in life with few material advantages, although his

French fashion plate of *c.* 1795

family was by no means indigent. His grandfather was a prosperous merchant and his father, William Brummell, had been private secretary to Lord North. This post brought him in touch with men as famous and fashionable as Charles James Fox and Richard Brinsley Sheridan, and George Brummell, even as a boy, must already have had a glimpse of the great world he was so soon to conquer. In 1790 he was sent to Eton where he was known as 'Buck' Brummell and where he established a reputation by his careful dress and his imperturbable *sang-froid*. He was sixteen when, in 1794, his father died. At Oxford he did not concern himself with what Barbey d'Aurevilly calls 'les laborieuses recherches de la pensée' but cultivated and extended his personal relations.

Accounts differ as to his first meeting with the Prince of Wales. According to one he was introduced by Lord Barrymore. According to another and more romantic story, the meeting took place at the thatched cottage which stood at that time in the Green Park, opposite Clarges Street. It was a kind of idealized farm (a sort of Petit Trianon in miniature) and George III had placed in charge of it a lady named Mrs Searle. She kept cows, perhaps not very seriously as she is said to have bustled about in a hooped skirt and high headdress in the style of the 1770s. It became the fashion for the Court ladies to call upon her, and on one occasion she was visited by the Marchioness of Salisbury, accompanied by the Prince of Wales. In the yard of the little farm the Prince fell into conversation with a handsome youth who was in fact Mrs Searle's nephew, George Brummell. 'And what do you wish to be when you leave college?' asked the Prince, and the young man replied that he would like to serve the King in the Army. He was immediately promised a commission in the Tenth Hussars, of which regiment the Prince was Colonel-in-Chief.

There is no doubt that His Royal Highness was immensely taken with his protégé; by his handsome face, his grace of carriage, his neat dress and by his easy conversation in which due deference was *pimenté* by the slightest hint of impertinence. It was exactly this piquant combination which won acceptance everywhere. It is true that such *bons mots* as have been reported do not seem to us to be very witty, but then wit is very much an affair of the occasion and of the personality of the speaker.

In any case Brummell soon found himself a welcome guest in the most exclusive circles, and it is not much of an exaggeration to say that from 1799 until 1810, at least, the fashionable hostesses competed for his presence, and that no party, no rout was complete without him. His behaviour, like everything else about him, was deliberately contrived. He soon gave up dancing, choosing rather to be a spectator, appearing for a few moments at a ball and then gliding away. 'Stay until you have produced your effect,' he counselled, 'and then go.'

He served in the Tenth Hussars for three years, rising to the rank of captain. But, by all accounts, he was a bad officer, completely indifferent to the welfare of his men and unpopular with his fellow officers, who envied his superior elegance and feared the sharpness of his tongue. When the regiment was posted to Manchester, he declared that no gentleman could bear to live in so barbarous a place and promptly resigned his commission. London, after all, was the only satisfactory stage for his performance. He was received everywhere and was a welcome guest at Carlton House until the day when he offended his host by some impertinence which went just a little bit too far.

Perhaps the famous story of the bell is apocryphal. 'Ring the bell, George,' Brummell is alleged to have said to the Prince; and when the lackey appeared he was told to 'order Mr Brummell's carriage'. But *si non e vero*, the tale is symbolically true of the delicate relations between the two men and of the perpetual tight-rope act which the dandy was compelled – or at least chose – to perform.

The Prince was very conscious of his growing corpulence. There was, as it happened, at Carlton House a very fat lackey known as Big Ben. Brummell not only referred to the Prince as

Big Ben but baptized Mrs Fitzherbert, who was also growing stout, as Benina. Such indiscretions were certain to be reported, and both the Prince and the lady were highly offended. Nonetheless, for a time, the Prince acted with great consideration for his protégé. On one occasion when Brummell presented himself at a ball (to which he had not been invited) he was met at the door by His Royal Highness himself who, it is said, 'gently urged him to retire, that he might not disoblige Mrs Fitzherbert.'

Considering the circumstances this was magnanimity indeed, and Brummell would have been well advised to accept the hand that had been offered to him. Instead he redoubled his sarcasms, and had the impudence to say to Colonel MacMahon (whom he knew to be in the Prince's confidence), 'I have made him what he is, and I can therefore unmake him.' This was not perhaps as utterly ridiculous as it sounds, for a considerable number of the aristocratic dandies were on Brummell's side, and Society continued to be amused whenever he seemed to have scored a point. One day, strolling down Bond Street with a friend, Brummell came face to face with the Prince on the arm of Lord Moira. His Royal Highness stopped to talk to Brummell's friend but pointedly ignored Brummell himself. As they parted Brummell was heard to murmur to his companion: 'Who's your fat friend?' It is needless to say that he was never again invited to Carlton House. However, the dandy continued to rule in the world of elegance, and made the fortune of his tailors, Davidson and Meyer, and of the glove-makers and cravat-makers who enjoyed his patronage.

In the memoirs of the period we catch vivid glimpses of him at this stage of his career. The famous Regency courtisane Harriet Wilson, meeting him at a party, tells us:

'He was extremely fair, and the expression of his countenance far from disagreeable. His person, too, was rather good; nor could anybody find fault with the taste of all those who, for years, had made it a rule to copy the cut of Brummell's coat,

The MACARONI PAINTER, or BILLY DIMPLE sitting for his PICTURE.

The Macaroni painter (mezzotint, *c.* 1780). The Macaronis of the 1770s and early 1780s were not dandies: their style of dress might be described as the last flourish of eighteenth-century artificiality before the dandy revolution.

Six 'Incroyables' of the Directoire period: etchings by Gatine after Horace Vernet

Left The French had now adopted a smartened version of English Country clothes for ordinary wear in Town; the riding boots, the tight breeches, the cutaway coat and the primitive form of top-hat all reveal the costume's derivation from sporting dress. *C.* 1814.

Centre Short frock coat, top-hat with flat brim, 'hessian' boots with metal heels, a coloured scarf as a neckcloth and a padded, piqué waistcoat. *C.* 1814.

Right Something 'incroyable' has indeed happened: the substitution of trousers for breeches. The despised *sans culottes* of the Revolutionary Period have at last come into their own – unless it was the influence of the Cossacks that put men into trousers. In any case this masculine costume was to remain unchanged in essentials for more than a century. *C.* 1814.

Left Formal attire, with nut-coloured breeches and stockings and pumps instead of riding boots, a white waistcoat and neck-cloth and a *bicorne* instead of a top hat. *C.* 1814.

Centre A closely tailored version of sporting clothes as ordinary wear. The *cravate aux oreilles* made every man look as if he suffered from goitre. *C.* 1814.

Right Although the name Incroyable was still retained, the extravagances of the Directoire period had now been abandoned, and the top hat had assumed its nineteenth-century form. In England the *bottes à la hussarde* were called 'hessians'. *C.* 1816.

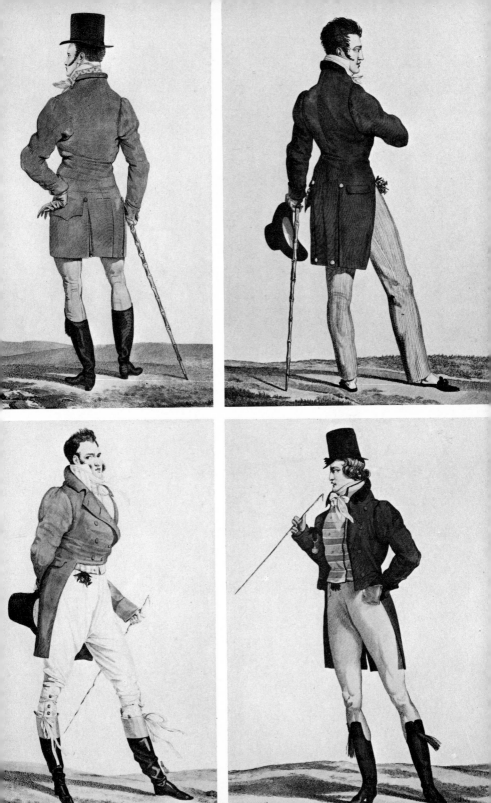

In Town in September, aquatint by G. C. Hunt. A dandy left in London at an unfashionable time, regretting his extravagant 'last Season'.

A caricature of the Directoire period, showing an *Incroyable* of the English country style. He is trying to heave up his breeches, which were now kept tight by means of braces, in contrast to eighteenth-century 'small clothes' which hung loosely from the hips.

the shape of his hat, or the tie of his neckcloth: for all this was in the very best possible style. "No perfumes," Brummell used to say, "but very fine linen, plenty of it, and country-washing. If John Bull turns round to look after you, you are not well dressed; but either too stiff, too tight, or too fashionable." In short, his maxims on dress were excellent. Besides this, he was neither uneducated nor deficient. He possessed, also, a sort of quaint dry humour, not amounting to anything like wit; indeed, he said nothing which would bear repetition; but his affected manners and little absurdities amused for the moment. Then it became the fashion to court Brummell's society, which was enough to make many seek it who cared not for it; and many more wished to be well with him, through fear, for all knew him to be cold, heartless and satirical.'

Nonetheless Harriet Wilson reports one remark of Brummell's which is surely to his credit. Someone having said, 'I vote for cutting all the grocers and valets who intrude themselves into good society,' Brummell replied, 'My father was a very superior valet, and kept his place all his life.'

From the *Reminiscences* of Captain Gronow we obtain other glimpses not only of Brummell but of the other dandies of his time. Chief among these was Lord Alvanley to whom were attributed all the *bons mots* circulating in the clubs 'after the abdication of the throne of dandyism by Brummell'. Another was Colonel Kelly of the Guards:

'He was very fond of dress; his boots were so well varnished that the polish now in use could not surpass Kelly's blacking in brilliancy; his pantaloons were made of the finest leather, and his coats were inimitable: in short, his dress was considered perfect. His sister held the place of housekeeper to the Custom-house, and when it was burnt down, Kelly was burnt with it, in endeavouring to save his famous boots. When the news of his horrible death became known all the dandies were anxious to secure the services of his valet, who possessed the mystery

Promenade dress:
sketch from the *Illustrated London News*, 1850

of the inimitable blacking. Brummell lost no time in discovering his place of residence, and asked what wages he required; the servant answered, his late master gave him 150 l. a year but it was not enough for his talents, and he should require 200 l.; upon which Brummell said, "Well, if you will make it guineas, I shall be happy to attend upon *you*". The late Lord Plymouth eventually secured this phoenix of valets at 200 l. a year, and bore away the sovereignty of boots.'

The physical aspect of the dandies can perhaps best be studied in Dighton's *Characters in the West End of the Town*, a series of charming etchings coloured by hand, also issued as a panorama, or continuous strip rolled into a neat little box. We can see Lord Yarmouth (afterward Marquis of Hertford and the original of Thackeray's wicked Lord Steyne), the Marquis of Londonderry, Lord Wilton, Lord Fife and Hughes Ball. We can watch Lord Alvanley 'going to White's'.

But Captain Gronow, who in his youth had certainly been one of them, could say, writing in 1850:

'How unspeakably odious – with a few brilliant exceptions such as Alvanley and others – were the dandies of forty years ago! They were a motley crew, with nothing remarkable about them but their insolence. They were generally not high-born nor rich, nor very good-looking, nor clever, nor agreeable; and why they arrogated to themselves the right of setting up their fancied superiority on a self-raised pedestal and despising their betters, Heaven only knows.'

Brummell himself was neither well-born nor rich, although he was certainly not poverty-stricken. His father is said to have left him £1,500 a year, a considerable sum in those days, sufficient to enable him to live the life of pleasure and to offer fine dinners to his friends, in his house in Chesterfield Street. His income might have sufficed until the end of his days, but for that passion for gambling which he shared with nearly all the Regency dandies. There was high play at all the clubs which had more or less recently been established in London: Arthur's, Almack's, Boodle's, Brooks's, Watier's and White's. The last two were Brummell's favourites and, apart from 'looking in at the Opera', he seems to have spent most of his evenings at one or the other. At first he was very successful and is said to have won £26,000 in one night, a sum equivalent to his entire fortune. But instead of investing it he lost it all a few evenings later.

The year 1814 was probably the turning point. London was full of young officers coming back from the wars, and foreigners of every kind eager to taste the pleasures of the capital. The gambling mania raged more furiously than ever. Brummell held on with varying fortune, but by the following year he had only a 'poor ten thousand guineas' left of his patrimony. He resorted to the money-lenders, but this only postponed disaster. In the spring of 1816 he realized that he was ruined and that the only course still open to him was to leave the country. On 16 May he dined for the last time at Watier's, and in a final attempt to stave off the inevitable he scribbled a note to his friend Scrope Davis, who, as it happened, was dining that evening in Charles Street with Byron – which is probably why we know about it. The note read:

'My dear Scrope, Lend me two hundred guineas. The Bank is shut, and all my money is in the Three Per Cents. It shall be repaid tomorrow morning. Yours, George Brummell.'

The reply was brought to him by messenger:

'My dear George, 'Tis very unfortunate, but all *my* money is in the Three Per Cents. Yours, Scrope.'

Brummell looked in at the Opera but did not stay for the end of the performance. Without returning home he got into a post-chaise and was driven at speed to Dover. Next day he was in Calais.

He took rooms over a bookshop near the Town Hall and with the thousand guineas which still remained to him he furnished his abode in style. He is said to have lived 'on credit', but how he

A DAY OF FASHION.

Sung with the greatest Applause by Mr. C. TAYLOR, at Vauxhall Gardens: Written, composed, and respectfully inscribed to
GEORGE ROGERS BARRETT, Esq., by Mr. W. T. PARKE.

In London's gay circle where pleasures abound,
  Away soon dull care makes his flight;
Each hour and each day is a merry-go-round,
  Still changing from morning till night.
In fashion's bright sphere time never stands still,
  They crow'd to the Op'ra or Play;
And like roving bees of life's sweets take their fill,
  While thus 'tis they make out the day.

(Spoken.)—In the morning, drop in at Christie's, to
see my Lord Squander sold off.—This, Ladies and
Gentlemen, is a portrait by Reynolds, and is considered to be his *chef d'ouvre.*—Bless me, says the Honor-
able Mrs. Squib, why that's the picture of Lady
Squander—My Lord's not going to sell that, I hope.—
Och! never mind, Madam, cries Colonel O'Bother,
you know it's no uncommon thing, now-a-days, for a
Man of Fashion to part with his Wife.—Five pounds
is bid—Six pounds, in two places—Seven—Eight—
Nine pounds—Nobody bid more—Going for nine
pounds!—One of the most beautiful and accomplished
Ladies—Going for only nine pounds!

(Sung.)—And sure no delights are so gay and so clever,
  'Tis London, dear London, for ever.

The morning amusements thus ended by five,
  The parties now homewards repair;
Make some calls, just to see if old friends are alive,
  Drop a card, at the multitude stare.
Arriv'd, to the toilette my Lady's seen pressing,
  Be quick, Betty, pray soon have done;
And after three hours are expended in dressing,
  Appears with scarce any clothes on.

(Spoken.)—Behold the party seated at the dinner-
table—Nine in the evening!—Pray, my dear Lady
Mary, was you at the Opera last night?—No, I was
not; my Lord was taken unwell, and I remained at
home to keep him company.—Lord! how unfashionable,
cries Mrs. Raccket—Well, for my part, I would not
have stay'd away from the Opera last night for all the
husbands in Christendom.—Oh, you should have heard
how divinely Signor Longuanti sung his Cavatina.—
Certainly persons of fashion would expire, if they had
not those dear Italians about them.—Pardon me,
Madam, says a truly noble English Duke, I think
they ought to expire, if, by giving their exclusive patronage to foreigners, they were to neglect the brilliant
talent possessed by those of their own country!

(Sung.)—And sure no delights are so gay and so clever,
  'Tis London, dear London, for ever.

The dinner now ended, the coffee gone round,
  They think how to finish the day;
What place best to go to, all voices resound,
  Vauxhall! where all's sportive and gay.
The coaches all ready, the guests enter in,
  They dash quick away, soon alight;
See all ranks most cheerful, and sure 'tis no sin,
  The eye, and the ear, to delight.

(Spoken.)—The gardens are thronged, the music
and singing enchanting, and the illuminations and
fire-works brilliant beyond description.—Waiter! says
Mr. Deputy Gobble, where's my chicken?—Pray,
Pappa, says Miss, let them *pull* a chicken or two for
us, they are but a few shillings dearer than the others.—
Thank you, my dear, says the Deputy, I can *pull*
them myself, and save that money.—Ah! Lady Canter,
cries Sir George Dash, do you sup here to-night?—
O dear no, Sir George, we are only come for a walk
after dinner, and are engaged to sup with Mrs. Allnight,
at six in the morning!—Waiter! bring half a dozen
jellies.—Waiter! Waiter!—Coming, Sir!—Bring another dish of ham!—And, d'ye hear—Take care you
don't cut it too thick, Sir!—Too thick, Sir! We have never
any complaints of that kind, I promise you!

(Sung.)—And sure no delights are so gay and so clever,
  'Tis London, dear London, for ever.

Published 24th August, 1813, by JAMES WHITTLE and RICHARD HOLMES LAURIE, No. 53, Fleet Street, London.
(The Music to be had of Mr. FENTUM, No. 78, Strand.)

'A Day of Fashion', by George Cruikshank, 1813

managed to do this for the fourteen years he remained in Calais
would be a mystery if he were not known to have been helped
by subventions from the Duke of Gloucester, the Duke of
Argyle, Lord Alvanley and the Duchess of York. He received a
stream of visitors, for Calais was the normal place to break the
journey to Paris, and these included the Duke of Wellington, the
Duke of Rutland, the Duke of Beaufort, Lord Sefton, Lord
Jersey and many others. Brummell received them with the
utmost hospitality – for which they were expected to pay
themselves.

And then, in 1821, 'Prinny', now King George IV, came in
person to Calais on his way to visit his other realm of Hanover.
In the midst of the crowd assembled to acclaim him he caught
sight of a familiar face and was heard to murmur, 'Good God!
George Brummell!' It is possible that a reconciliation might
have been effected but Brummell was too proud to do more than
add his name to the visitors' book at the hotel. Next day the
King had departed and the chance was gone.

Brummell had hoped to be made British Consul but it was
not until 1830 that the Duke of Wellington appointed him
Consul, not at Calais but at Caen. This post was more or less
a sinecure and Brummell was still able to enjoy some sem-
blance of civilized leisure. But, two years later, he was dismissed
by Lord Palmerston, and soon fell into poverty. He was indeed
imprisoned for debt in 1835 and only rescued by an appeal to
his friends in London. His mind gradually gave way; he was
admitted to the Caen Asylum and died on 30 March 1840.

To the Victorians he was the very type to point a moral if not
to adorn a tale, yet Brummell cannot be merely dismissed as an
example of a wasted life. Was it wasted? Byron declared that
the three greatest men of his time were Napoleon, himself – and
George Brummell. Certainly he stood – as Wilde was to claim
to do later – in a 'symbolic relation to his Age'. And, equally
certainly, it is impossible to think of the Regency without think-
ing of him. We have noted the impact he had on the Society of

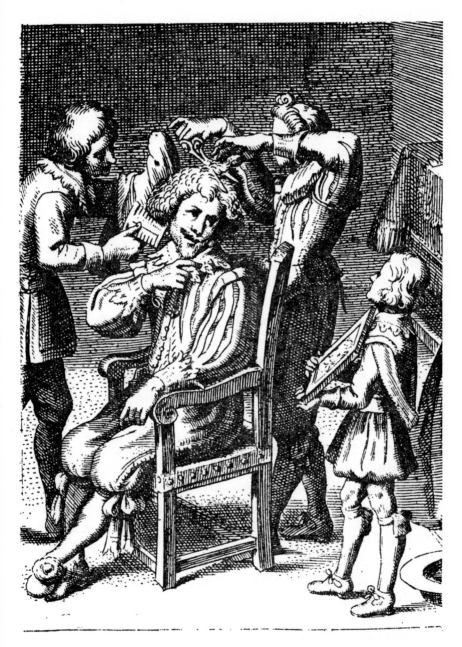

The narcissist. Seventeenth-century engraving by Van Horst

his time. What was the interior mechanism of his psychology?
Without plunging too deeply into the mysteries of psycho-
analysis, it is perhaps helpful to consider him as a narcissist.
The simplest form of narcissism involves the display of the
naked, or near-naked body; but this original, crude exhibitionist
tendency tends to be sublimated by being displaced on to clothes.
However, when we have said this we are only at the beginning
of the problem; for the natural expression of exhibitionism in
dress would seem to lie in the direction of more gorgeous clothes,
and for long periods of human history this was the case. Dandyism, however, as we have seen, is the *repudiation* of gorgeous and
conspicuous attire; and this cannot entirely be explained by
the fact that, according to Flügel and other workers in this field
of social psychology, 'women are, perhaps by nature and certainly
in virtue of our social and sexual traditions, more narcissistic
than men.'

We take it for granted, as Flügel says, that 'an amount of time
and energy devoted to clothes that would be considered excessive
in a man might be regarded as normal in a woman.' It might be
thought a logical consequence that the 'very high degree of
narcissism characteristic of the dandy is usually correlated with
some degree of sexual abnormality (or at any rate a relative
incapacity for normal hetero-sexual object love).' There is no
evidence that Brummell, whatever sexual abnormality was
present in his make-up, was a homosexual. On the other hand
he certainly showed indifference to women.

The only liaison (which may have been no more than a 'senti-
mental attachment') of which we have any hint was, rather
surprisingly, with the Duchess of York. It is said that they
corresponded, and Mary Craven, in the Introduction to her
translation of Boutet de Monvel's *Beau Brummell and his Times*,
tells us that 'M. Armstrong, the Caen grocer, who displayed such
generosity to the fallen favourite, possessed a gold snuff-box and
casket full of love letters written to Brummell by a lady of high
rank. After M. Armstrong died, a mysterious stranger arrived in

Beau Brummell, anonymous stipple engraving. The portrait has all the marks of authenticity and must have been taken from the life. It is all here: the handsome features, the good-humoured arrogance, the hint of impertinence, the complete self-possession, and of course, the immaculate cravat.

Drawn ... Dighton Jan.t 1819

Going to WHITES.

Beau Brummell, etching and mezzotint by Robert Dighton, 1805. Dark blue cutaway coat with metal buttons, 'hessian' boots, fawn-coloured breeches, beaver hat and elaborate neckcloth: the style which was to impose itself on every gentleman in the first decade of the nineteenth century.

Opposite An etching of Lord Alvanley, by Richard Dighton. Lord Alvanley was one of Beau Brummell's friends and rivals. His witty remarks were sometimes credited to Brummell, and vice versa. Alvanley was 'going to White's' to gamble, as Brummell did too, to his final ruin.

The GOLDEN BALL.

Etching by Richard Dighton, 1819. Hughes Ball was another well-known dandy of the period. His costume is a striking answer to those who imagine that dandyism had something to do with gorgeousness in dress. In fact his clothes might almost be those of an undertaker.

Etching by Richard Dighton, 1822. Fat Nugent, as Harriet Wilson calls him in her *Memoirs*, was the half-brother of Henry Luttrell, natural son of the second Earl of Carhampton. Luttrell was a well-known conversationalist and diner-out and the author of *Advice to Julia: a letter in Rhyme.*

A VIEW of NUGENT.

Caen and claimed the snuff-box and the casket, doubtless acting on the instructions of the writer, who knew that the letters existed, and desired the records of her intrigue to be destroyed.'

This is little enough and is certainly in striking contrast to the uninhibited eroticism of most of the Regency dandies. Perhaps we shall best understand Brummell by regarding him as a narcissist *pur sang*, a man who loved only himself. Why then should the self-satisfaction expressing itself in his clothes result in garments so consistently unostentatious?

Flügel, attempting to classify the psychological male types with regard to their attitude to dress, distinguishes what he calls the 'self-satisfied type'. He calls him a 'clothes prig' and suggests that the excessive self-satisfaction of such a person is a defence mechanism against extensive feelings of inferiority, an 'exaggerated positive self-feeling' which has attached itself especially to clothes. Flügel sees as the basis of this a strong castration complex, a desperate clinging to 'a satisfaction in clothes, because these, in virtue of their phallic symbolism, give reassurance against the fear of phallic loss.'

Be that as it may (and we can be certain that Brummell himself would hardly have begun to understand the language of modern psycho-analysis), we can possibly find a clue here to the dandy's unconscious motivation, his reaction against a feeling of inferiority on two counts. The first would be his sexual inadequacy, expressing itself in his indifference to women; and perhaps this would explain the entire absence of feminine suggestion in the clothes he chose to wear. Not for him the lace ruffles and other female fripperies of the macaronis of a previous generation. His clothes (tightened and smartened, it is true) were those of the English sporting squire.

This compensated for his feeling of inferiority on the personal level. But he must also have felt inferior on the social level. It is true that he did not exactly spring from the lower classes: his father had been sufficiently wealthy to send him to Eton, but the world in which he finally established himself included the cream of the British aristocracy, a society which, at that time, was not at all welcoming to the *parvenu.*

Perhaps we shall best understand the importance of Brummell if we realize that the revolution he symbolized was essentially a *conspiracy against aristocracy.* Brummell saw instinctively that the day of aristocracy was over and that the day of gentility had arrived. There were to be no more peers wearing their Orders proudly on their embroidered coats, but only gentlemen in plain cloth and immaculate linen. There were to be no more be-plumed and gold-laced *tricornes*, but only well-brushed top hats. The top hat was indeed a symbol of the new dispensation. On this flat but exalted plateau, it seemed to say, all gentlemen are equal, even if one of them is called George, Prince of Wales, and the other is called George Brummell. Indeed there was nothing to distinguish them except that Brummell's cravat was more carefully tied and his coat better fitting.

Fit, in fact, was the new fetish. Norah Waugh, in her pioneering book *The Cut of Men's Clothes, 1600-1900,* gives an admirable summary of what had happened.

'Whereas the eighteenth century was characterized by its attention to cut, the nineteenth was notable for its concentration on fit . . . This state of affairs was due to several causes, the main one being the adoption of cloth and a more scientific approach to the whole technique of tailoring . . . The fashionable coat of the 1770s hung loose from the chest, for it was not possible to fit the coat to the body with only two side seams placed so far back . . . If, however, the coat was cut in cloth, a much more pliable material than tightly woven silk, shrinking and stretching by the tailor's iron could mould it and give it a more subtle fit, even if the coat was worn buttoned. By the end of the eighteenth century English tailors became the leaders of men's fashions, because their long experience of the subtleties of cloth had developed their skill and they gave style and elegance to the practical country coats

'Jeune Noble', French fashion plate of 1789

and so made them acceptable for fashionable wear. Beau Brummell, not an innovator but a perfectionist, set the seal on the new fashion by removing the odour of the stables. He had the floppy cravat starched, the muddy boots polished and above all, he demanded perfect cut and fit.'

He was indeed such a perfectionist that he had his coats made by one tailor, his waistcoats by another and his breeches by a third. He is even said to have patronized two glove-makers, one for the thumb and one for the rest of the hand. And the trouble he took with his cravats has become proverbial. The story has often been told of a morning visitor to Brummell who found him being dressed by his valet. On the floor was a large heap of crumpled cravats. The visitor inquired what they were and the valet answered: 'Sir, those are our failures.'

The cravat was a large square of linen, muslin or silk folded diagonally into a band and starched. It was wound round the collar attached to the shirt, and the top of the collar appeared above it. An alternative form of neckwear was the stock, a band of horsehair or buckram, sometimes edged with leather and fastened at the back with a buckle, or hook and eye. It is obvious that the effect of both cravats and stocks was to constrict the throat and hold the head rigid, thereby giving the look of *blasé* indifference which was expected of the perfect dandy. Only sometimes the constriction was so extreme that the face was empurpled and the eyes seemed to be about to pop out of the head.

Of course, Brummell himself never countenanced such extravagancies. There is a sense in which his real successors were not the dandies but the ordinary well-dressed English gentleman. And this at least can be said of Brummell, that he dictated the main lines of male fashion to the whole of Europe for the next hundred years.

London Publish'd by W. S. Fores So Piccadilly Aug.ᵗ 9ᵗʰ 1817

...d Angelic pon honor—fascinating Creature
...onstrous handsome !! D—m me if she isn't
Divinity !!! for further particulars enquire of the Original.

A Dandy, 1817. Anonymous etching coloured by hand. The caricaturists
were beginning to find in the dandies a fine subject for ridicule. An
interesting feature of this early example is that breeches and stockings
have begun to be replaced by tights.

The DANDY CLUB.

Above The Dandy Club, etching by Richard Dighton, 1818. This print, like the others by Richard Dighton, is from his *Characters at the West End of Town*. There is a degree of caricature here which he did not allow himself in his named portraits.

Opposite The Hobby Horse Dealer, etching coloured by hand, by George Cruikshank after 'J. S., Esq.', 1819. The dress of the three dandies is contrasted with that of the 'horse dealer'. Two at least of them are wearing tights and one the wide 'cossack' trousers with understraps. The spurs must have been an encumbrance as the machine was propelled by pushing with the feet.

A Dandy, anonymous etching, *c.* 1820. The final stages of the dandy's toilet. As he is attired for the evening and is wearing tights and pumps he will presumably choose the *bicorne* rather than either of the top-hats.

Monstrosities of 1819 & 1820,
etching coloured by hand by George
Cruikshank. An exaggeration, but
not very much so in the case of
the male figures. Nearly all the
gentlemen are wearing trousers,
those of the lancer tight, those of
the others voluminous. The man
on the right is wearing spurs –
and carrying an umbrella!

Monstrosities of 1825 & 1826,
etching coloured by George
Cruikshank. Another scene in
Hyde Park, this time in winter.
The trousers are now very strange,
tight over the knees and baggy
elsewhere. The top-hats are
somewhat higher in the crown
than those of two or three years
before.

Modes de Paris. Fashion plate from the *Petit Courrier des Dames*, July 1835. The sporting outfit shown is unlikely to have made much appeal to Englishmen. The 'correct' fashion is purely English, although white duck trousers were probably more frequently seen in Paris than in London.

The Author of 'The Exquisites', anonymous etching, *c.* 1835. The author of this satire on dandyism was the Spanish dramatist Don Trueba y Cosio (1805–35). The style of dress is that of the middle 1830s when evening dress had assumed the form it has kept with few variations to this day.

His most Gracious Majesty George the Fourth, engraving by George Cruikshank, 1821. 'Prinny', who has come to the throne at last, attired in the evening clothes of dandyism, but only just able to squeeze into them. He is said to have burst into tears when Brummell told him his breeches did not fit.

Portrait of Baron Schwitter by Eugène Delacroix. The portrait is of interest as showing how completely the European aristocracy had, by the 1830s, assimilated English modes. The Baron has even adopted the funereal overtones made fashionable by that 'blighted being', the author of *Pelham*.

2

The second generation: Bulwer, Disraeli, D'Orsay

If Brummell was the typical dandy (but, indeed, he was more than typical, he was *the* type) of the Regency period, Bulwer may well be taken as the typical dandy of the next generation. He was born in 1803 and when he came of age, the older man had already been in exile for eight years. It is true that his fame, and his influence, lived on, but the dandyism of the new age was different in some essentials from that of the old.

Perhaps the difference can be summed up in one word: Romanticism. No one could have been less romantic than Brummell. For him dandyism was not only an expression of his own nature but a means of entering Society and cutting a figure in it. Bulwer had no need to *enter* Society. Although his origins were not quite so grand as he liked to think, he was sufficiently well-connected to find no difficulty on that score. He was also, unlike Brummell, an intellectual and, if not quite a genius, at least a man of enormous talent. He also had enormous industry and enormous ambition.

He was little more than a schoolboy when *Ismael, an Oriental Tale; with other Poems by Edward George Lytton Bulwer* was published in 1820. Of course the work is derivative, under the obvious influence of Byron and with echoes of Scott, who first, says the young author, 'inflam'd me with a Poet's fire'. Bulwer himself later dismissed it with contempt, but at least it was an earnest of things to come; and the formidable Dr Parr was moved to write that 'when I think of your youth, my delight is mingled with astonishment at your intellectual powers'. And Dr Parr was noted for the severity of his judgments.

We are not, however, concerned with Bulwer's early writings.

Portrait of Bulwer by Daniel Maclise, 1832

He himself considered 'Ismael' to be too obviously Byronic, all 'thronged with bulbuls and palm-trees', and repudiated his first novel *Falkland* almost as soon as he saw it in print. It was about the doomed scion of a decadent race living in a Gothic ruin who 'feasted upon the passions' and gave himself up to 'gloomy reflections'. His next work was of an entirely different kind.

Michael Sadleir, in his penetrating *Bulwer: A Panorama*, draws an interesting parallel between the period immediately following the Battle of Waterloo and the period immediately after the First World War. Both were times of social upheaval, the break-up of the old social categories, a frenzied search for pleasure and for the means to pay for it. 'Everything that glittered,' says Sadleir, 'might not be gold; but most things, provided they glittered sufficiently, served for currency.' Nothing was 'of importance to the still aspiring elegant beside the conviction that, if he tried hard enough, he too might join the elect . . . The most popular routes to social prominence lay through sport, the fashionable "hells", scandal and literature.'

Literature! That was something Brummell had never thought of; but, as we have seen, Bulwer had been engaged in some form of literary composition from his earliest years. And now, just at the right moment, there arose a school of writing which tried to reflect the glitter of contemporary life, to produce what was known as the 'fashionable novel', or 'silver-fork fiction'. 'It served,' says Sadleir, 'as a kind of Court Circular for the ambitious, as a textbook in etiquette for the parvenu, as a means of pin-money for clever society women, and as an outlet for the satiric bile of well-connected *révoltés*.' It gave pleasure to two different sections of the public: those who were outside Society but were thus enabled to flatten their noses, so to speak, against the windows and see what was going on inside, and those who were themselves inside and could recognize many of the characters depicted. For it goes without saying that nearly every 'fashionable novel' was a *roman à clef*. In fact, its one virtue was verisimilitude, with an attempt to describe not only the actions and emotions of the characters but their clothes and furniture. Its vogue lasted for little more than a decade, so that Bulwer was fortunate in bringing out *Pelham* in 1828.

The publisher of such works was Henry Colburn, who had a genius for spotting best-sellers, and, against the advice of his readers, decided to publish *Pelham, or the Adventures of a Gentleman*, prophesying that it would be the book of the year. And after a slow start, he was proved right: the book was so successful that people began to speak of a 'Pelham' when they meant a dandy.

There is no doubt that *Pelham* was a considerable advance on anything that Bulwer had previously written, and he had not yet acquired, to any marked degree, those baroque convolutions of language which were to disfigure his later works. He did not yet think it necessary to refer to fishing as 'the gentle craft of the Angle', to call windows 'admittants of the celestial beam', or a jug and wash-basin 'the appurtenances of lavation'. The style of *Pelham* is straightforward, concise and witty. Some of the epigrams have dated, but not all. In fashionable life of almost all periods it would be true to say: 'Nothing, my dear sir, is like a liaison with a woman of celebrity. In marriage a man lowers a woman to his own rank; in an *affaire de coeur* he raises himself to hers.'

Some of the dialogue anticipates Wilde, as when Lord Vincent implores Pelham to lay aside his natural levity, as he has something important to say to him. Pelham replies: 'My lord, there is in your words a depth and solemnity which pierce me through one of N's best stuffed coats, even to the very heart. Let me ring for my poodle and some *eau de Cologne* and I will hear you as you desire.'

Contemporaries were delighted with such sallies, and those in the know were able to recognize many of the outstanding personalities of the time. It was plain that the elegant young author had actually *been* to some of the great houses, such as Hatfield, and was familiar with their decorations and furnishings. And he was a perfect guide to what a dandy should wear. The book even had one quite important effect on the history of dress. Until then, evening coats could be dark blue or plum colour. Pelham's was black, and black evening coats have been ever since.

Bulwer complained that people insisted on considering his hero as a picture of himself, having said exactly the same about Falkland, a gloomy romantic personage not in the least like Pelham. The truth would seem to be that both the characters embodied something of their author. If he could be as frivolous as Pelham, he was also capable of considering himself, like Falkland, a 'blighted being'. In fact, that is supposed to be one of the reasons why he introduced black evening coats, in mourning, as it were, for lost innocence and youth: the Byronic pose of having arrived, prematurely, at the 'sere and yellow leaf'.

The reactions of the critics varied enormously. Sir Walter Scott, always generous, described the style as 'easy and gentleman-like'. Lockhart, Sir Walter's son-in-law, admitted that 'I have not read the book from disliking the author,' whom he described as 'a Mr Bulwer, a Norfolk squire and a horrid puppy'. Carlyle became quite hysterical with rage. He wrote to the editor of *The Edinburgh Review* that novels like *Pelham* ought to be 'extinguished'. He attempted to do the extinguishing himself in the pages of *Fraser's Magazine*, and returned to the charge in *Sartor Resartus*, in the chapter entitled 'The Dandiacal Body':

'Among the new sects of England one of the most notable is that of the Dandies . . . They have their Temples, whereof the chief, as the Jewish Temple did, stands in their Metropolis and is named Almacks . . . Nor are sacred books wanting to the sect; these they call Fashionable Novels. Of such sacred books I, not without expense, procured myself some samples and in hope of true insight and the zeal which beseems an Inquirer into Clothes, set out to interpret and study them. But wholly to no purpose.'

4

He could not read them to the end because 'magnetic sleep soon supervened'. If Carlyle had really been an 'Inquirer into Clothes', and not merely concerned to emphasize the scandalous difference between the luxury of a dandy and the poverty of an Irish peasant, he might have found much meat for meditation in the pages of *Pelham*, as well as in those of another young author who was just coming into prominence.

There is a curious parallelism between the early careers of Bulwer and Benjamin Disraeli. The two men knew each other and remained on friendly terms, although the friendship was never as close as that between Bulwer and Benjamin's old father, Isaac D'Israeli. Long before he had met him Bulwer had admired D'Israeli senior's book which appeared in 1818 under the title *The Literary Character illustrated by the History of Men of Genius*, and was much influenced by it in his own *England and the English*.

In the puff which Colburn, the publisher of both Bulwer and Benjamin Disraeli, inserted in the *New Monthly Magazine* (which he owned: it was very useful for him to be able to push his own wares in his own critical journal), he described the hero of *Vivian Grey* as 'an ambitious, dashing and talented young man of high life'. The description might serve not only for Disraeli's hero and Bulwer's Pelham, but for the young authors themselves. Both were practitioners of the 'society' novel, both had political ambitions, both were dandies.

At first, however, Disraeli had to contend with more prejudice than Bulwer, and when it was discovered that the author of *Vivian Grey* was 'Mr D'Israeli, junior' – a Jew, in short, and unlikely to be very conversant with the habits of high society – a torrent of vituperation descended on his head. It was even suggested that he had obtained his material from the private diaries of men more fashionable than himself. A modern writer, Ellen Moers, whose study, *The Dandy* is a monument of research, states bluntly that Disraeli was 'the one Regency novelist who had no knowledge at all of the exclusive world of which he wrote.' For that matter, neither had Balzac, and if Disraeli had not the genius of Balzac he had enough acuteness of observation, helped out with a little bluff and bluster, to make a convincing picture.

Disraeli had little formal education, and although his family was prosperous enough, his father's circle consisted of scholars and literary men. It was not among these that he could have met a Vivian Grey. He was articled to a firm of solicitors in 1821 and through the hospitality of the partners, was introduced to a wider circle, but it was still merely respectable upper middle-class. In these surroundings he was long remembered for his 'rather conspicuous attire', 'a black velvet suit with ruffles, and black stockings with red clocks'. This would certainly not have earned the approbation of Brummell and, indeed, Disraeli's dandyism had always something a little baroque about it, a touch of the exoticism which was part of his nature.

A few years later when he had come to know Bulwer, he appeared as a guest at one of the latter's parties in 'green velvet trousers, a canary coloured waistcoat, low shoes, silver buckles, lace at his wrists'. On other occasions he wore purple trousers with a gold stripe down the seam, a scarlet waistcoat, gold chains, a profusion of rings (he even wore rings over his white gloves), and he had 'long black ringlets framing his markedly Semitic features'. With all this went a mouth set in 'a sort of half-smile, half-sneer'. He was referred to as 'that damned bumptious Jew boy' and many people disliked him intensely.

Disraeli did not care. His object (the opposite of the true dandy's) was to be as conspicuous as possible, to be, as it were, his own trade-mark, and in this he undoubtedly succeeded. He had at least made sure that people did not forget him, and it was probably owing to his social notoriety that he managed to get a foothold in politics – although it is true that he had to try five times before he was elected to Parliament, and that when he made his first speech there his appearance evoked nothing but hostility and ridicule.

The shedding of his eccentricities and the maturing of mind and character which were finally to lead him to the highest point of political life is not our theme, although we may note, in passing, the extraordinary way in which the political career of Vivian Grey anticipates that of Disraeli himself. He insinuated himself into the confidence of the Marquis of Carabas and tried to form with him a party first to embarrass and finally to overturn the Government. Yet Disraeli had not yet met Lord George Bentinck, still less formed that strange alliance of 'the Jew and the Jockey' which was later to play quite a conspicuous part in the English political scene. And it is surely extraordinary that Vivian Grey, visiting Château Désir (a revealing name!) should meet there a peer bearing the as yet non-existent title of – Lord Beaconsfield. But the young Disraeli had a long way to go before he really moved in these exalted circles.

If we are looking for a third figure typical of the second generation of dandies we can hardly fail to choose Count d'Orsay. Rather perversely Barbey d'Aurevilly denies that d'Orsay was a dandy, because he was something much more, 'une nature infiniment plus complexe, plus ample et plus humaine que cette chose anglaise'. He was too amiable, and amiability is a sentiment entirely foreign to dandyism. Be that as it may, it was surely men like Bulwer and Disraeli who were 'much more' than mere dandies. They did something with their lives whereas d'Orsay, in spite of his charm and his talents, did little except to acquire a reputation as the most elegant man of his time.

Perhaps one should not include d'Orsay in this chapter at all but save him for the next, which is concerned with dandyism in France. But if he was by birth a Frenchman he lived a considerable part of his life in England, and, in the words of Ellen Moers, 'carried dandyism back and forth and back again across the Channel'.

D'Orsay was an authentic Count, in the sense that his forbears, in the eighteenth century, had purchased a country estate which carried the title with it: there was nothing unusual in this

From a caricature of George Bentinck by Count d'Orsay

under the *ancien régime*. He had also among his ancestors a
Flemish princess, an Italian dancer and a German duke. He
became allied to the highest French nobility by the marriage of
his sister to the Duc de Guiche, son of the Duc de Gramont, and
he came to England for the first time when the latter was sent as
Ambassador Extraordinary to the coronation of George IV.

D'Orsay was then twenty years old, and immediately found
himself accepted by London society; in fact he became at once
à la mode. He was well-bred, charming, generous (although it
must be confessed that his generosity was frequently exercised
with other people's money), above all he was gay. He was an
expert *metteur en scène*: he would arrange the menu of a dinner
party with as much effortless *expertise* as he used to fascinate
the guests. He won over the most unlikely people, such as
Carlyle and Tennyson. In short he was irresistible. It is true that
some prudish people disapproved of the curious *ménage à trois*
which he set up with Lady Blessington – or was it a *ménage à
quatre*, since he was married to her daughter? It is true that
there were times when he could only go out at night for fear of
being arrested for debt. Such things never displaced a curl on
that Apollonian unwrinkled brow.

There are a surprising number of descriptions of d'Orsay's
clothes in contrast to the few we have of Brummell's. But perhaps this is not so surprising after all. For once one has recorded
that Brummell's coat was blue (and a perfect fit), that his cravat
was immaculate and carefully folded, and that his boots were
well-polished, what more is there to say? Brummell himself
would not have wished for more; but d'Orsay is another matter.

Through the eyes of such very different people as Benjamin
Haydon the painter, Jane Carlyle and Lady Holland, we can
build up a composite picture. Haydon was quite overwhelmed
by the splendour of 'such a dress – white greatcoat, blue satin
cravat, hair oiled and curling, but of the primest curve and
purest water, gloves scented with eau de cologne, or eau de
jasmine, primrose in tint, skin in tightness.' Jane Carlyle's reac-

tion was a mixture of astonishment and mockery on seeing 'the fantastical fineness of his dress: sky-blue silk cravat, yards of gold chain, white French gloves, light drab greatcoat lined with velvet of the same colour, invisible inexpressibles, skin-coloured and fitting like a glove.' How, one might ask, if his 'inexpressibles' were invisible, did the lady know that they fitted like a glove? Lady Holland was frankly hostile towards his costume, 'which is composed of sky-blue pantaloons and other strange mixtures. He wears his shirt without a neckcloth, fastened with diamonds and coloured stones – in short a costume that *men* disapprove as effeminate and nondescript.' Unlike ladies, *men*, perhaps, would have hesitated to call d'Orsay effeminate; he was well over six foot and broad in proportion. He was also a formidable duellist. Lady Holland suffered from the common nineteenth-century delusion that fine or gorgeous clothes on men are *necessarily* effeminate.

And she is surely wrong about the absence of neckcloth. Nearly all other observers declare that d'Orsay usually wore one of black satin, not starched like Brummell's but soft and rippling in the wide V of the waistcoat. The waistcoat was a very important item, for he wore his coat thrown back so as to expose it, and it was looped across with gold chains which made it even more conspicuous. His waving hair and curling whiskers completed the picture.

Perhaps he was seen to best advantage on horseback. He was a superb rider, although his horsemanship suggested the riding school rather than the hunting field. He even inspired verse, although it was only the verse of Bernal Osborne:

> 'Patting the crest of his well-managed steed,   –
> Proud of his action, d'Orsay vaunts the breed;
> A coat of chocolate, a vest of snow,
> Well brush'd his whiskers, as his boots' below;
> A short-napp'd beaver, prodigal in brim,
> With trousers tighten'd to a well-turn'd limb . . .'

When he rode in the Park he did so 'to the admiration of all beholders, for every eye is sure to be fixed upon him'. And from another contemporary account, Captain Gronow's, we learn that

'from the colour, and the tie . . . of the Kerchief which adorned his neck, to the spurs ornamenting the heels of his patent boots, he was the original for countless copyists, particularly and collectively. The hue and cut of his many faultless coats, the turn of his closely-fitting inexpressibles, the shade of his gloves, the knot of his scarf, were studied by the motley multitude with greater interest and avidity than objects more profitable and worthy of their regard, could possibly hope to obtain. Nor did the beard that flourished luxuriantly upon the delicate and nicely-chiselled features escape the universal imitation. Those who could not cultivate their scanty crops into the desirable arrangement, had recourse to art and stratagem to supply the natural deficiency.'

The 'inexpressibles' (the early Victorians simply could not bring themselves to utter the word trousers) were, indeed, trousers, strapped under the instep, and not the riding breeches of the previous generation.

D'Orsay's end, like that of most dandies who are nothing else, was rather sad. He had the sense to keep up with the times and to modify, as he grew older, the extravagancies of his earlier costumes. That acute observer Jane Carlyle gives what is in effect two pictures of him, at five years' interval:

'13 April 1845 – To-day, oddly enough, while I was engaged in re-reading Carlyle's *Philosophy of Clothes*, Count d'Orsay walked in. I had not seen him for four or five years. Last time he was as gay in his colours as a humming-bird – blue satin cravat, blue velvet waistcoat, cream-coloured coat, lined with velvet of the same hue, trousers also of a bright colour, I forget what; white French gloves, two glorious breast pins attached by a chain and length enough of gold watch-guard to have hanged himself in. To-day in compliment to his five more

Fashion plate, *The Gazette of Fashion*, c. 1820. The long overcoat was much affected at this period, when one of the most fashionable diversions was driving four-in-hand, as it could be very cold 'on the box'. The top hat, very wide at the top, shows one of many possible shapes.

A Dandy, anonymous lithograph, *c.* 1835. This has been said to be a portrait of Eugène Sue, the prolific French writer, author of *The Wandering Jew* and other sensational popular novels. If so it provides an interesting example of the gradual sobering-up of the French dandy's costume, for it is in striking contrast with the next plate.

Eugène Sue. Anonymous lithograph, *c.* 1840. The dandy has now shaved his moustache and wears only the 'Newgate Fringe', and his costume, including the neckcloth, is of unrelieved black. The hat too has assumed a very austere form.

A portrait by Count d'Orsay, 1839, of Prince Louis Napoleon, the future Emperor Napoleon III. When in exile in London he affected the dress of the dandies, and was the personal friend of many of them, including d'Orsay himself.

Un habitué du boulevard des Italiens, lithograph by Gaverni, *c.* 1840. The famous boulevard was much frequented both by men about town and by the more successful journalists, and this would seem to be one of the latter. He is to some extent *en déshabille*, i.e. wearing a kind of housecoat.

years, he was all in black and brown – a black satin cravat, a brown velvet waistcoat, a brown coat some shades darker than the waistcoat, lined with velvet of its own shade, and almost black trousers, one breastpin, a large pear-shaped jewel set in a little cup of diamonds, and only one fold of gold chain round his neck, tucked together right on the centre of his spacious breast with one magnificent turquoise . . . A bungler would have made no allowance for five years more at his time of life, but he had the fine sense to perceive how much better his dress of to-day sets off his slightly enlarged figure and slightly worn complexion, than the humming-bird colours of five years back would have done.'

A fashion historian would feel impelled to add that d'Orsay showed a sense not only of his own maturing but of the progress of the century, for men's dress was to become more and more sombre during the next decade and after. D'Orsay was only forty-four when Jane Carlyle limned this portrait. He had seven more years to live. He died in Paris on 4 August 1852, and was buried at Chambourcy under the same monument as Lady Blessington. Most of the obituary notices lamented his passing with obvious sincerity. The malicious Count Horace de Viel-Castel, however, was more critical, especially of d'Orsay's artistic pretensions:

'D'Orsay had no talent; his statuettes are detestable and his busts very bad . . . He died ten years too late, for he became at last merely a ridiculous old doll.'

Certainly the kind of dandyism he stood for had outlived its mode. But perhaps we may leave the last word to Dickens:

'D'Orsay, by all who knew him well, is affectionately remembered and regretted, as a man whose great abilities might have raised him to any distinction, and whose gentle heart even a world of fashion left unspoiled.'

Not many dandies have received such an epitaph.

5

Portrait of d'Orsay by Maclise

3
The Dandy
in France

D'Orsay, as we have noted, was accepted as a supreme dandy both in England and in France, but the French saw behind him the figure of Brummell who was not French at all. They had been aware of him in his great days, and could not be unaware of the influence he still exerted after his exile and even after his death.

It is one of the curiosities of social history that the French, so completely convinced that there is no culture but French culture, so chauvinistic, so provincial even, in their estimate of what goes on outside France, should yet suffer from recurring bouts of what they themselves recognize, by the name they give it, as a kind of madness, namely anglomania. It raged in the 1790s, in the *Directoire* period, and the fact that the two countries were at war for nearly twenty years seems to have made no difference to the admiration which Frenchmen felt for the Englishman's clothes. When contact was re-established in 1814, and again in 1815, after the brief interlude of 'the Hundred Days', it became plain that if Englishwomen decided, once for all, to adopt French fashions, French men were equally determined from then on to dress *à l'anglaise*, with the nagging suspicion that, try as they would, they were not quite managing to do so.

The *Restauration* had brought back the Bourbons, but it did not succeed in bringing back the clothes of the *Ancien Régime*. Louis XVIII himself dressed, except on state occasions, like an English country gentleman; Charles X likewise, and Louis-Philippe like a prosperous English merchant, for the bourgeois king had no pretensions to dandyism. Yet his reign, from 1830 to 1848, was the very period when the French dandy was most in evidence; and the French, with their passion for ideas, tried to explain, in intellectual terms, what it was all about.

From a French fashion plate showing men's costume in 1819

The man who introduced dandyism into France as a philo-
sophic concept was the poet Barbey d'Aurevilly, whose book
Du Dandysme et de Georges Brummell appeared in 1844. The
image he presented of Brummell was, he said, 'the statuette of a
man who did not deserve much more than a statuette'. In the
political history of England Brummell had no place, but in its
social history it was a different matter. He was an expression
of those social tendencies which historians neglect at their peril
and, as such, well worth the study of serious persons. Barbey
d'Aurevilly regretted that he had the pen neither of a Stendhal
nor of a Montesquieu to do the subject justice. He managed,
none the less, to come to some pretty profound conclusions.

Dandyism, he saw, was on the one hand a trait of the universal
vanity of mankind, but, on the other, something local and par-
ticularized. In a word, it was a trait of *English* vanity; and that
was why the French, having no word of their own for it, were
compelled to adopt the English term. He even went so far as to

say that there were no true French dandies, only pale imitators of their English counterparts.

That Barbey d'Aurevilly concerned himself with dandyism and above all with English dandyism was the result, in Ellen Moers' happy phrase, 'of a curious series of literary, psychological and geographical coincidences, tracing back to the early eighteen-thirties, when four ill-assorted gentlemen found themselves in Caen.' The first was Brummell, who arrived there in 1830 to take up his duties as British Consul; the second was a young English lieutenant, William Jesse, who came in 1832 to recuperate from service in India; the third was a native of Caen named Trebutien; and the fourth was Barbey d'Aurevilly, who had been sent by his parents to Caen in order to study law.

During the year he spent in the Norman city Barbey d'Aurevilly met neither Jesse nor Brummell, although he persuaded himself later that he had *seen* Brummell. Trebutien, however, knew Jesse, and before he left Caen in 1833, Barbey d'Aurevilly had struck up a friendship with Trebutien; and it was owing to the latter's good offices that Barbey d'Aurevilly was able to enter into a correspondence with Jesse, who was already collecting materials for his life of Brummell, which did not actually appear until 1844. All that Barbey d'Aurevilly knew about Brummell he obtained from Jesse; which does not mean that Barbey's book is valueless. For if Jesse's book is an invaluable repository of the facts, *Du Dandyisme et de Georges Brummell* is the work of a philosopher and a poet.

A much greater poet than Barbey d'Aurevilly was to take up the same theme. Baudelaire's essay on Constantin Guys was first published in 1863 as a series of *feuilletons* in *Le Figaro*, and his literary reputation ensured that they appeared shortly afterwards in book form, in a work entitled *L'Art Romantique*. It is curious that Baudelaire, in his essays, does not even give the name of the artist he was writing about; he refers to him as 'M.G.', i.e. Monsieur Guys. This was probably in deference to the almost morbid modesty of the artist himself who shrunk from any kind of publicity and never even signed his drawings. He even broke off relations with Thackeray who during a visit of Guys to London (he did many drawings for *The Illustrated London News*) had been so indiscreet as to refer to him by name.

Constantin Guys is now regarded as one of the most valuable pictorial commentators of the mid-nineteenth century and his pen-and-wash drawings are highly prized. He was himself, at least in his youth, a dandy, and, in addition, as his biographer P. G. Konody remarks, 'a lover of women and horses, a keen student of the pageantry of life during the Second Empire'. No one has depicted more convincingly the elegance of the man-about-town, preferably on horseback or driving a tilbury or phaeton. And he drew military men with inimitable *panache*.

Baudelaire deals with every aspect of his output, but the chapter which interests us most is the one devoted to the theme of 'The Dandy'. He begins by saying:

'The rich, lazy man who, even though he be blasé, has no other occupation than to follow the trail of happiness; the man who has been brought up in luxury and who from his youth has been accustomed to the obedience of other men; he, finally, who has no other profession than elegance, will always, in all periods, enjoy an appearance altogether apart and distinct. These beings have no other lot than to cultivate the idea of the Beautiful in their persons, to satisfy their passions, to feel and to think. They have thus at their disposal, and in a large measure, the time and the money, without which imagination, reduced to the state of a passing reverie, can scarcely be translated into action . . . If I have spoken of money, it is because money is indispensable to people who make a cult of their passions; but the dandy does not aspire to money as an essential thing; indefinite credit would do as well for him; he leaves this gross passion to vulgar mortals. Dandyism is not even, as many rather thoughtless people seem to believe, an

A sketch by Degas of Barbey d'Aurevilly

immoderate taste for dress and material elegance. For the perfect dandy these things are only a perfect symbol of the aristocratic superiority of his spirit.'

If one were to quarrel with a single word of this acute analysis, it would be with the word 'aristocratic', for it is the theme of the present study that aristocracy and dandyism are not at all the same thing, and are even sometimes diametrically opposed. Baudelaire himself seems to recognize this, for he goes on to admit:

'Dandyism appears especially in the transitory periods when democracy is not yet all-powerful, and when aristocracy is only partially unsettled and depreciated. In the confusion of such periods, some few men who are out of their sphere, disgusted and unoccupied, but are all rich in natural force, may conceive the project of founding a new kind of aristocracy ... Dandyism is the last splendour of heroism in decadence ... Dandyism is a setting sun; like the star in its decline, it is superb, without heat and full of melancholy. But alas! the rising tide of democracy, which invades and levels everything, drowns day by day these last representatives of human pride and pours the flood of oblivion over the traces of these prodigious Myrmidons. The dandies are becoming rarer and ever rarer with us, whilst with our neighbours in England, the social order and the Constitution (the true Constitution which is expressed by manners) will long continue to find a place for the heirs of Sheridan, of Brummell and Byron, as long as there are claimants worthy of it.'

It would seem that Baudelaire thought of himself as a dandy, although if the two requisites for dandyism are leisure and money, he had, for the greater part of his life, plenty of the first and very little of the second. But he boasted that even in the depths of his poverty, he had never spent less than two hours on his toilet, and Brummell himself could hardly have spent more.

Certainly in his youth he had the reputation of a dandy. He

Robert Houdin, woodcut from *L'Illustration*, 1845. Robert Houdin was the most famous conjurer of his day and gave performances 'before all the crowned heads of Europe'. He always appeared in 'immaculate evening dress', which we can see here in the form it had already assumed before the middle of the century.

Four scenes of Parisian life, *c.* 1860, by Constantin Guys. Guys was a prolific illustrator with an extraordinary feeling for the chic of the period, and he produced a vivid series of pictures of the life of the second Empire. *Below opposite* shows a military review, with all the panache of cavalry, particularly of the Hussars.

Baudelaire. Photograph, c. 1855. Baudelaire was the philosopher of dandyism but it is doubtful if he was ever a dandy himself. His life was largely spent in the company of bohemians and to them he may have seemed dandified simply because he washed. Brummell would certainly never have passed *that* for a neckcloth.

The Duc de Morny, woodcut by M. Chenu, c. 1860. The Duc de Morny was the illegitimate son of the Comte de Flahaut and Queen Hortense, and he was therefore the half-brother of Napoleon III. His evening dress, the neckcloth having shrunk to a modest 'white tie', is almost indistinguishable from that of modern times.

wore his hair long and sported a moustache and a beard; his
clothes were well-made and in the prevailing fashion. But he did
not belong to the dandies' world; his friends were the literary
men of the Left Bank. He was a dandy among bohemians, and
he remained so even when he had changed entirely his style of
dress. This change was reflected chiefly in an abandonment of
all colour, even of the red cravat and rose-pink gloves he had
previously worn. He now wore nothing but black, shaved off his
whiskers and close-cropped his hair. He was, he explained, in
mourning for the age in which he had the misfortune to live.
It is curious that both Bulwer and Baudelaire, who both thought
they were expressing a personal reaction, should in fact have
been anticipating the clothes which were to be worn for the
second half of the century. How they would both have hated
the idea! The last thing they wished for was to dictate the
clothes of the bankers and business men of the next generation,
who had no 'aristocracy of spirit', did not regard themselves as
'blighted beings' and were not at all 'in mourning' for a period
of increasing trade and industrial expansion which suited them
so well.

Meanwhile the real dandies, the *jeunesse dorée* of the Second
Empire, tripped along the primrose path in complete ignorance
of the philosophizings of Baudelaire and Barbey d'Aurevilly. The
pursuit of pleasure was their only occupation, an occupation
strenuous enough to bring some of them to an early grave. Chief
among these martyrs was the Duc de Gramont-Caderousse, the
acknowledged chief of what was called '*la haute noce*', that is,
dissipation on the grandest scale. He ran through an enormous
fortune and died at thirty-two, leaving nothing to his heirs, said
the gossips, but a wardrobe containing a pierrot costume, a
Breton costume, a costume of the period of Henri IV and one of
Louis XIII. He was passionately fond of fancy dress. But it
would be strange if the wardrobe contained nothing else for he
was one of the most celebrated dandies of his day. His extreme
good looks, the perfect fit of his clothes, his immense *faux col*

6

(for the collar had by this time superseded the cravat) were as famous as his English carriages, his English grooms and his English dogs. If anyone suffered from anglomania it was certainly he. He passed his days at the races or driving in the Bois and his evenings at the Café Anglais or the Maison Dorée where he and his boon companions made merry with the most celebrated *grandes cocottes* of the period. Sometimes there were violent quarrels over the rival charms of these ladies, but Gramont-Caderousse was always able to get out of a scrape by his wit and his charm. He was a kind of d'Orsay with perhaps a little extra touch of persiflage and impertinence. He treated women like Anna Deslions and Blanche d'Antigny with a mixture of courtesy and irony which his contemporaries thought delicious. But he did not confine his amours to the demi-monde; known to be the lover of the Duchesse de Persigny, he made a bet that he would leave on her shoulder the visible trace of a kiss. When the lady appeared at a dinner the following evening in a décolleté gown, those in the know were able to perceive that the mark was well and truly there. When the Duke expostulated, Gramont-Caderousse drew himself up and said, 'Monsieur le Duc, I will not permit you to speak ill of my mistress.'

Persigny was one of the architects of the *coup d'état* and an intimate of Napoleon III. Another was the Duc de Morny, the illegitimate son of Queen Hortense and therefore half-brother of the Emperor. He was a dandy, but a dandy with a difference, who only pretended to be a playboy. He was a Don Juan, a large operator on the stock market, a wit, an epicure and a leader of fashion. His manner was cool – almost with that *phlegme britannique* which was one of the marks of the dandy – and, it was noted, he 'affected to treat a matter of state in a careless, disdainful fashion and to concentrate his mind on a farce, a menu, or a cravat.' He was tactful and courteous when he chose and made an admirable President of the Legislative body, but he was completely ruthless in his suppression of opponents of the régime he had 'founded, served and dishonoured'.

A sketch of Charles Dickens by Maclise, 1839

He provides an interesting parallel with and contrast to his English contemporary the Marquis of Hertford who, since he spent most of his time in Paris, can usefully be considered here. Living on his Irish rents (and contributing not a farthing to the relief of the Irish famine) he was, like Morny, cool, cultivated and impeccably dressed. But while Morny's dandyism was a mask for more sinister activities, Hertford lived only for pleasure. One should perhaps add that that pleasure included the acquisition of one of the most remarkable private collections of pictures and furniture ever got together. How can the moralist judge between these two men? Morny almost *created* the Second Empire; but, a few years after his death it had collapsed in ruin. Hertford's art treasures are what we know as the Wallace Collection, so perhaps his time was better employed after all.

It is perhaps natural that, especially in the second quarter of the nineteenth century, novelists should either *be* dandies or aspire to be so, or failing both, should depict a type they so much admired. We have already studied Bulwer and Disraeli, and if we have omitted Dickens it is because his dandyism never succeeded in making him more than a 'gent'; and even *his* imaginative range never succeeded in creating a really convincing specimen of the upper classes. In France, the same might be said of Balzac, whose personages are most convincing when they are drawn from the curious half-world of aspiring ambition and doubtful expedients to which the great novelist himself belonged.

We know from contemporary records that he himself aspired to be a dandy and that when he arrived to try his fortune in Paris in 1830 he owed his tailor a sum which would have sufficed to maintain him for a year. He professed to possess a different waistcoat for every day of the year, and as many pairs of gloves. The buttons on his coat were gold (or, perhaps, silver-gilt) and curiously chased, his enormous walking stick had a head studded with jewels. He had the honesty, or the cynicism to admit that all this, like the extraordinary clothes of the young Disraeli, was

French fashion plate captioned 'Lequel est
le plus ridicule!' showing costumes from 1760–1849

intended to serve as an advertisement, and this motive, as we
have noted, is the antithesis of true dandyism.

Certainly, once people had seen Balzac they never forgot him.
He never passed unnoticed, although the reaction to his fantastic
appearance was never very favourable even among those who
admired his genius. Captain Gronow tells us that,

> 'the great enchanter was one of the oiliest and commonest
> looking mortals I ever beheld; being short and corpulent,
> with a broad florid face, a cascade of double chins, and straight
> greasy hair . . . Balzac had that unwashed appearance which
> seems to belong to French *literati*, and dressed in the worst
> possible taste, wore sparkling jewels on a dirty shirt front,
> and diamond rings on unwashed fingers.'

Yet Balzac took dandyism very seriously and his early work in
journalism (for such papers as *La Silhouette* and *La Mode*) was
almost entirely concerned with such subjects as '*Physiologie de
la toilette*', '*Etude de moeurs par les gants*' and '*De la Cravate
considerée en elle-même et dans ses rapports avec la société*'. He
even published a whole *Traité de la vie elégante*. Whether the
real dandies of the Jockey Club paid any attention to these
dissertations may well be doubted, but Balzac was not aiming at

them. He divined that dandyism had nothing to do with the survivors of the *ancien régime* but was a technique – a weapon almost – in the hands of the new aristocracy of enterprise and talent. He pretends to have met Brummell, which he certainly never did, and to have heard from the great dandy's own lips what he calls the 'immortal sentence' that if people are struck by your appearance, you are not well dressed. It is curious that his own practice should have been so much at variance with this admirable precept.

It goes without saying that a novelist like Eugène Sue was far below Balzac in genius, but his personal dandyism was more authentic, even to the extent of winning the approval of Captain Gronow. He was received into the best society, had his own elegant English carriage, and was a personal friend of d'Orsay, who is said to have been the model for his *Marquis de Létorière*. In *Arthur* he pictures himself in the role of a dandy. Indeed it might be said that while Balzac studied dandyism in order that he might write novels, Sue wrote novels in order that he might continue to be a dandy on the proceeds of their sale. Still, they were not mere pot-boilers. They present a convincing, and even terrifying picture of the Paris of their period, its luxurious *hôtels*, its sordid slums – and of the people who dwelt in both. His novels, indeed, are due for a revival; they are at least as good as Bulwer's: they tell a good story and are not disfigured by the Englishman's intolerable affectations of style.

Not only writers but painters aspired to dandyism. The correct attire of a Delacroix and the careful *toilette* of a Gavarni were in strong contrast to the bohemian tradition of the art schools and *ateliers*. But as the century passed its half-way mark it was plain that they were, to some extent at least, survivors from an earlier epoch. Louis Napoleon himself had been something of a dandy during his London exile. As Emperor, his clothes were hardly distinguishable from those of the Prince Consort. For the time being, in England and in France, the day of the dandy was over.

Engraving by Bosse from *Le Jardin de la Noblesse Française*, 1629

4
The Enemies of Dandyism

Dandyism has never lacked enemies, but we are not here concerned with Carlyle and the 'anti-dandiacals', who in articles in *Fraser's Magazine*, in pamphlets and in books, directed the onslaught of the 1830s and 1840s on dandies in general and on the 'fashionable novels' in which their life was depicted. When we reach the second half of the century *that* particular conflict is over. The war of the moralists against dandyism had been more or less won, and the whole world of men, aristocrats as well as merchant bankers, had settled down to a drab uniformity of attire in which every manifestation of personal eccentricity was condemned as bad form.

Behind this lay the idea that there was something morally reprehensible in a man who paid too much attention to his own clothes. In its more extreme form the protest had an Evangelical form, for Evangelicalism in one of its aspects was nothing more than the re-emergence of seventeenth-century Puritanism. A man might suggest the purity of his thoughts by clean linen but he must also show the seriousness of his mind by the sombre line of his clothes. By the middle of the nineteenth century most Englishmen had come round to this point of view, at least so far as the outward man was concerned. The newly prosperous bourgeoisie was probably quite sincere in its convictions but even the aristocrats conformed in dress, however free their private behaviour might be. In such a climate it is difficult to see how the dandy could flourish or how his social prestige could be maintained.

However, in the period from 1860 to 1890 dandyism had other foes, the more dangerous in that they staged no frontal

Max Beerbohm, by Will
Rothenstein. Beerbohm in his
Oxford 'dandy days': well-fitting
lounge suit and stiff all-the-way-
round collar fashionable in the
1890s.

A photograph of Joseph Chamberlain, *c.* 1875, then a rising politician who was extremely conscious of his clothes. Note the tape-edged silk-faced coat, the loose tie confined in a ring, and the monocle, which became his characteristic mark.

The Marquis of Hartingdon, cartoon by 'Ape' in *Vanity Fair*, 1869. The correct dress for a politician with aristocratic connections. The caption reads, 'His ability and industry deserve respect even in a man: in a Marquis they command admiration.' He afterwards became the eighth Duke of Devonshire.

Opposite Fashion plate from the *Tailor and Cutter*, 1876. Men's clothes have now 'fossilized' almost completely. What was originally a crash-helmet for the hunting field has now become a fragile silk hat, spotted and spoilt even by a shower of rain. The frock coat and the morning coat have become *de rigueur* and the striped and 'shepherd plaid' trousers are completely formal. Only the boy's costume offers a touch of fantasy.

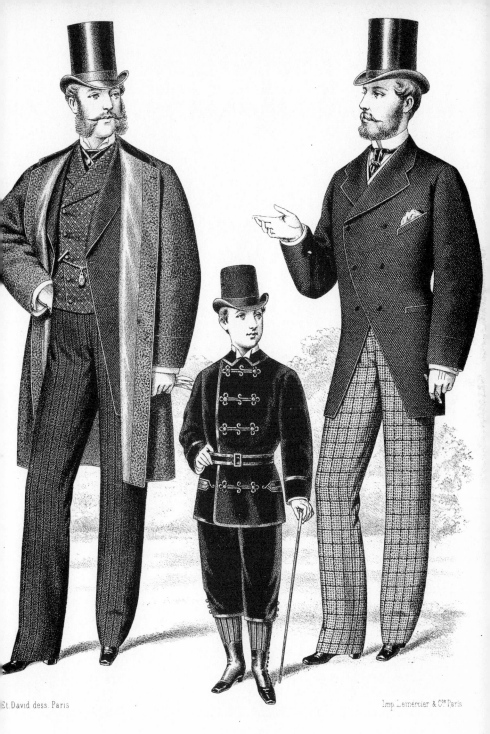

PORTRAIT GALLERY OF BRITISH·COSTUME
Spring 1876

El.David dess. Paris

Imp. Lemercier & Cie Paris

Published with the " TAILOR AND CUTTER " by John Williamson, *93 Drury Lane London W.C.*

James McNeill Whistler. Sketch for the caricature by 'Spy' in *Vanity Fair*, 1880. Like Joseph Chamberlain, Whistler wore a monocle and to do so was almost to proclaim oneself a dandy. Certainly Whistler was very conscious of the fit of clothes and wore them with an air.

attack, indeed, made no overt assault at all, but by sapping and mining gradually undermined the whole structure, even if most of them were unconscious of what they were doing.

The first of these foes was sport. Now the clothes worn by Brummell were themselves sporting clothes. They were simply a version of late eighteenth-century hunting costume, tightened and smartened for wear in Town. This seems to be the process by which all men's clothes develop. They start by being sports costume, they are then adopted, and adapted, for ordinary day wear, they then become evening dress and, if they run through the whole gamut they end as servants' costume. It is obvious that the mid-nineteenth-century footman was wearing the discarded clothes of the eighteenth century, just as the modern waiter wears the discarded clothes of the nineteenth. The whole process might be described as beginning in formalization and ending in fossilization.

At the period we are considering the clothes which had originally been designed for sport (i.e. hunting) had reached such a degree of formalization that they had become unsuitable not only for work (*that* they were always intended to show) but for any kind of active pursuit. The Victorians were just beginning to realize that the top-hat was not a very practical headgear for playing cricket, still less for rowing in the Oxford and Cambridge Boat Race. Nor – although many men continued to wear it – was it very suitable for long country walks; nor was the frock coat in heavy broadcloth which went with it.

Riding was still the dominant sport during the first half of the century and this involved very little modification, but when cricket became ever more popular, when football was increasingly played at the public schools and, most of all, when tennis arrived, it was obvious that new sports clothes would have to be invented. The cricket costume was, so to speak, ready made. The early nineteenth-century cricketers merely took off their coats and waistcoats, and the white shirt, still often frilled and with a collar, was worn with white duck trousers which were usual wear for

Manners and Customs of ye Englyshe (New Series) No. 2.

A Fashionable Club.   four o'clock p.m.

Caricature from *Punch*, 1850

the summer. It is true that the early nineteenth-century cricketers continued to wear a top-hat, and did not trouble to conceal their braces. Apart from these differences cricket costume has remained the same ever since; and so, until quite recent times, has men's tennis costume.

The real invention, for country pursuits, was the lounge suit, usually made of tweed or some other patterned material and worn with a bowler hat. The same cloth was used for the short coat as for the waistcoat and trousers, which is the reason why the outfit is called a 'suit' in English and a '*complet*' in French. The bowler hat had a low, rounded crown. William Coke of Norfolk is said to have invented it, and at Locke's hat shop in St James's Street it is still referred to as a 'William Coke hat'. In popular parlance this became a 'billycock'. The first examples were actually made by a craftsman named Bowler, and this was the name which finally stuck to this new kind of head-gear.

As can be seen from contemporary fashion plates, men's clothes, by the early 'eighties, had divided into two: on the one hand the black frock coat with checked or striped trousers, a black or white waistcoat and a silk hat; on the other a lounge suit worn with a bowler. It goes without saying that no gentleman would wear the second of these two costumes in Town. To walk down Bond Street in mid-morning or stroll in the Park on Sunday in anything but frock coat and top-hat would have been unthinkable. It is a curious example of what seems the inevitable development of men's clothes that the lounge suit finally formalized itself into the modern 'correct' wear of the City banker. But in its early form, however well-cut, it gave very little scope for dandyism of any kind. The country gentlemen of the 1870s and 1880s therefore did something to destroy the ideal which had been set up by their counterparts of nearly a century before. Some daring spirits went so far as to wear the 'Norfolk' jacket with knickerbockers and, for yachting, monkey jackets, pilot coats and reefers of blue serge.

The other influence tending to destroy the dandy ideal was that of the Aesthetic Movement. We are not here concerned with its effect on female costume. Anyone turning over the pages of *Punch* of the 1880s is familiar with the flat shoes, the uncorseted figure and the loose robe with wide sleeves, vaguely derived from Renaissance costume. Some aesthetic ladies adopted what they imagined was a version of Greek dress, but of course they did not really drape rectangles of cloth about their bodies but had the draperies sewn on to ordinary clothes, the final effect being hardly distinguishable from contemporary fashionable dress.

Their male counterparts wore a costume consisting of knee breeches, velvet jacket and a loose flowing tie; and it was this outfit which excited the contempt and ridicule of all right-thinking men. *Punch* made itself the champion of Philistine common sense and, in the drawings of George du Maurier, lost

YE GORGEOUS YOUNG SWELLS!

YE ÆSTHETIC YOUNG GENIUSES!...

no opportunity of ridiculing the Aesthetes. Then Gilbert and Sullivan took up the theme and the enormous success of *Patience* in 1881 – with the hero, Bunthorne, dressed in the aesthetic costume – did much to stamp the image on the public mind. Hints for the character of Bunthorne were taken partly from Whistler and partly from Oscar Wilde, and it is interesting to note that the producers of the play hardly succeeded in distinguishing one from the other.

We must try to disentangle the two threads. Whistler, by his enthusiasm for blue china, oriental fans, peacock's feathers and the like, his doctrine of beauty for its own sake – sliding over into 'art for art's sake' – had certainly done much to promote aesthetic enthusiasms. Indeed, he was regarded as the inspirer of the new movement. And then, in 1878, Oscar Wilde came down from Oxford where he had already acquired a reputation as the Apostle of Aestheticism. In 1882 he set out on a tour in America with a lecture rather pretentiously entitled 'The Practical Application of the Principles of Aesthetic Theory to Exterior and Interior House Decoration, with Observations upon Dress and Personal Ornaments'. And he was dressed in

what for the sake of convenience we may call the Bunthorne costume.

In his lecture he complained that the modern world had 'lost all nobility of dress', especially in the costume of the male.

'Perhaps one of the most difficult things for us to do is to choose a notable and joyous dress for men. There would be more joy in life if we were to accustom ourselves to use all the beautiful colours we can in fashioning our own clothes. The dress of the future, I think, will use drapery to a great extent, and will abound in joyous colour.'

Certainly the ordinary fashionable men's dress of the 1880s was neither notable nor joyous. But had male costume ever been so? Yes, indeed!

'I think we may be pardoned a little enthusiasm over the dress of the time of Charles I, so beautiful indeed, that in spite of its invention being with the Cavaliers, it was copied by the Puritans. And the dress for the children of that time must not be passed over. It was a very golden age for the little ones.'

This last opinion had the unfortunate result of condemning a whole generation of small boys to be dressed in the costume of Little Lord Fauntleroy. But what the late Victorians were glad to accept as a costume for children they were unable to accept as a suitable attire for grown men.

Whistler had no patience with such opinions; indeed he very soon lost patience with Wilde himself. He had begun by regarding him as a disciple, but Wilde did not see himself in that light. Hence the friction between the two men, which culminated in acid exchanges in the Press. Whistler would never admit that Wilde knew anything about art at all, and referred to him as 'the amiable, irresponsible, esurient Oscar – with no more sense of a picture than of the fit of a coat.'

This was indeed to hit the nail on the head, for Whistler undoubtedly thought of himself as a dandy, even as a military

Three scenes from the programme for *Patience*, 1881

dandy (had he not been at the Military Academy of West Point?) and his slim figure carried off a well-fitting coat to perfection. He would have nothing to do with the uniform of the Aesthetes, however 'notable and joyous' it might be. For dandyism must eschew exoticism either of time or place. Wilde had no such inhibitions, and if he went back to the seventeenth century for his general effect he went abroad for his overcoats. Whistler had seen him alighting from a hansom in a long green overcoat *à la polonaise*, 'marvellously befrogged and befurred', and wrote (through the medium of the Press, of course) begging him to 'restore those things to Nathan's, and never again let me find you masquerading the streets of my Chelsea in the combined costume of Kossuth and Mr Mantalini.'

This was sound advice, for the dandy can never have anything to do with exoticism; he must never seem to be in fancy dress. But perhaps there was not so much difference between the two men after all. Both were using costume as a means of impressing an image of themselves on the public mind, but even in this Whistler showed more shrewdness than Wilde; for it is important that the public image should always be the same. Whistler wore a silk hat but it was of unusual form with a flat brim all the way round; and in summer he wore white duck trousers – a fashion which was still valid in America but had gone out in England a generation before. He habitually wore patent leather pumps, sometimes with coloured bows, enough in itself, one would have thought, to single him out from the ordinary man-about-town. Occasionally, in evening dress, he had a salmon-coloured silk handkerchief protruding from his waistcoat and, when a friend tried to push it out of sight, exclaimed, 'What are you doing? You've destroyed my precious note of colour.' Whistler, in short, never quite succeeded in looking, and perhaps would not have wished to look, like an English gentleman. It is very revealing that when, on one occasion, staying at the seaside, he asked the landlady what she thought he was, she replied, 'I should fancy you was on the 'Alls.' There was, in short, some-

'The original "Champagne Charlie" '

thing theatrical about him; but to say this is not at all to equate
Whistler with the whole race of pseudo-swells familiar to music
hall audiences, the 'Champagne Charlies', the 'Shoreditch
Toffs', the 'Burlington Berties of Bow'. None the less, he was
always, so far as London Society was concerned, a little bit out
of the picture. Wilde, on the other hand, conformed. Abandon-
ing altogether the Aesthetic outfit of his youth, he appeared in
the 1890s in the immaculate frock coat and shiny silk hat of his
fashionable contemporaries. It is with these that we must deal
in the next chapter.

5

La Belle Epoque and since

La belle époque is a more convenient phrase than 'the Edwardian Period'; the latter lasted a mere decade while the former may be said to cover almost a generation, from about 1890 to the outbreak of Word War I. And it is justifiable both for England and France for, so far as the upper classes were concerned, the English Channel had almost ceased to exist. They were as much at home at Deauville and 'Monte' as at Ascot and Cowes. Riding or driving in the Bois was indistinguishable from riding or driving in Hyde Park. The whole epoch has been called 'the Casino and Garden Party Period', the 'Age of Extravagance' and 'Hig' Lif's Last Fling'. Certainly it saw a real revival of dandyism.

The underlying causes were not so dissimilar from those operating in the first age of the dandies. An old aristocracy was being replaced by a new plutocracy, and it is in such periods that the dandy has a chance to flourish. Those of the old order who continued to hold their place did so by reason of their wealth; but they no longer formed an exclusive Society. In England, the King himself set the example. His most intimate friends were the Duke of Devonshire, the Marquis de Soveral and Mr (later Sir) Ernest Cassel: that is an aristocrat, a foreign diplomat and a Jewish financier.

But if the strands which made up Society were mixed, a visitor from Mars at any fashionable gathering might have come to the conclusion that all the men were obeying some sumptuary law which compelled them to dress alike. He might, perhaps, have noted a slight difference between the frock coat and the morning coat (the *Tailor & Cutter* remarked in 1898 that the morning coat had lately become 'more popular than it has been for years') and a small degree of fancy in the waistcoats. The shiny silk hat was, of course, absolutely *de rigueur*.

A writer in the same informative journal (writing in 1890) declares:

> 'A crack West End tailor told me that a smart man has a fresh coat for every day of the week. He will start the season with about twenty suits costing about five guineas each. The crack price for an evening suit is £20. Thrice each day does a fashionable man array himself; a tweed suit is his morning wear; in the afternoon he dons a Frock coat, a smarter waistcoat and a bigger tie. In the evening he dresses for dinner. Perhaps his dinner clothes will be exchanged for a smoking suit later ... The middle-class young man on £15 [presumably on an income of £15 a week] gets about four new suits a year.'

It was very important to know exactly *when* to wear the right clothes, as any departure from the norm was regarded as a social *gaffe*. The *London Tailor* rather tartly tells its readers that 'it is an error for gentlemen to go to public dinners or to assemblies *where ladies are present*, in dinner jackets; and yet they will do it.' A tail-coat was considered necessary for dining in any smart restaurant, except in the 'Grill Room' (where only men were present). Most gentlemen put on a dinner jacket to dine at their club. In the theatre, full evening dress was expected in the stalls and at least a dinner jacket in the 'Dress Circle' – a phrase which so oddly persists into our own day.

London was undoubtedly the arbiter of correct masculine costume, as even fashionable foreigners realized, although (the *Tailor & Cutter* admits) 'much beautiful work is turned out in Paris'. The waistcoat assumed an importance it had not had since the days of the early Victorian dandies. Discretion however was needed. The admirable journal from which we have been quoting rather grudgingly admits that 'the somewhat obtrusive checks or the birdseye spots on a blue ground have

THE "REX"
TAILOR-MADE SHIRT.
PERFECT FIT GUARANTEED.

White, all Linen Fittings, 4/6 ... ... 6 for 26/-

   „   Fine Linen Fittings, 5/6 ... ... 6 for 32/-

   „   Extra Fine Linen, 7/6 ... ... 6 for 42/-

   „   Dress Wear, 5/6, 7/6, 9/6.

   „   Specialite Pure Linen Shirt, 10/6.

Advertisement from the *Illustrated London News*, 1890

been the favourite patterns of the modern fancy waistcoat'; but it issues a rather portentous ukase against looking 'of the horse horsey'; and remarks: 'The sprigged and flowered waistcoats of our grandfathers may be revived but gentlemen with abdominal convexity will use discretion in the employment of hues and patterns calculated to draw attention to that unromantic formation.' A timely warning, since in that age of 'English' breakfasts and five-course lunches and seven-course dinners and muffins and cakes for tea (to say nothing of a cold chicken snack in the middle of the morning or late at night) there were quite a number of gentlemen who suffered from 'abdominal convexity', including the Monarch himself.

King Edward VII, even while still the Prince of Wales, had always been very careful of his dress and was regarded as a model of sartorial correctness, not only in England but in France and America. As early as the late 1860s, he had had several garments called after him, such as the 'Albert Top Frock' and the 'Albert Driving Cape'. Americans continued to call a frock coat an 'albert' long after this; but in England the word had long been obsolete and became incomprehensible when the new King decided to call himself Edward VII instead of Albert I as Queen Victoria wished.

English public men and members of Parliament (with the notable exception of Mr Gladstone) had always been rather well dressed by comparison with their Continental counterparts, but in the 1880s and 1890s new standards of sartorial elegance were set, notably by Lord Randolph Churchill and Mr Joseph Chamberlain, who with his immaculate frock coat, lustrous silk hat, monocle and the inevitable orchid in his buttonhole was the admiration of political friends and foes alike. Dandyism was once more of good repute.

The dandy begins to appear once again in literature after a long eclipse. Oscar Wilde regretted that the 'fashionable novel' had ever fallen out of favour and that the 'brilliant young dandies in whom Disraeli and Bulwer Lytton took such delight, have

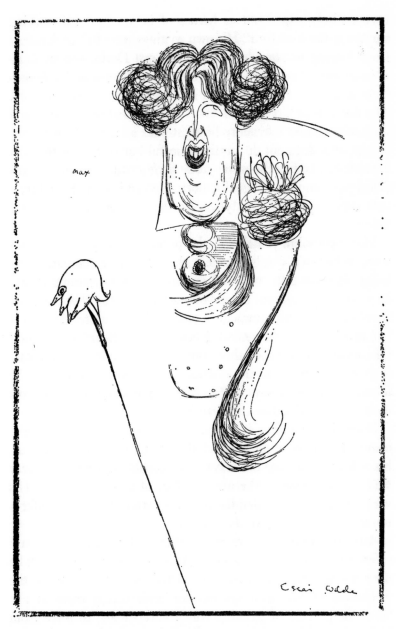

A sketch of Oscar Wilde by Beerbohm

been entirely wiped out as heroes of fiction by hard-working curates in the East End'. His own writings were full of dandies: Lord Goring in *An Ideal Husband*, Lord Darlington in *Lady Windermere's Fan*, Lord Illingworth in *A Woman of No Importance* and Lord Henry Wotton in *The Picture of Dorian Gray*. The doctrine of 'art for art's sake', the repudiation of moral and utilitarian values, inevitably brought back an admiration for the dandy, who does not do anything useful but is content to 'exist beautifully'. In fact the whole *fin de siècle* attitude implied a dandiacal pose, and it was equally inevitable that it should produce a new philosopher of dandyism, in the person of Max Beerbohm.

Max Beerbohm remains in the public memory as an author who, in his own words, 'made a charming little reputation' by using his small gifts 'well and discreetly, never straining them'. In 1898 he brought out a thin volume entitled *The Works of Max Beerbohm* with the comment 'I shall write no more. Already I feel myself a trifle outmoded. I belong to the Beardsley period.' Of course he did write other books which delighted an increasingly large public, but the essence of Beerbohm is already to be found in the four essays in *The Works*. The one which concerns us is entitled 'Dandies and Dandies'.

Beerbohm was himself a dandy, *fin de siècle*, with all the fragile charm the phrase implies. His clothes were always beautifully cut, his silk hat lustrous, his cravat impeccable, and he knew very well how to manage 'the nice conduct of a clouded cane'. His very prose style was dandiacal. Who better than he to offer a miniature philosophy of dandyism?

After rehearsing once more the story of Beau Brummell, and referring to Carlyle and Barbey d'Aurevilly (strangely enough he does not mention Baudelaire) he criticizes d'Orsay not for the feebleness of his paintings but for undertaking them at all: 'It is the process of painting which is repellent; to force from little tubes of lead a glutinous flamboyance and to defile with the hair of a camel therein steeped, taut canvas is hardly the

Oscar Wilde. Photograph by
G. Savony, 1882. Whistler always
denied that Oscar Wilde was a
dandy and indeed in these early
days he affected an 'aesthetic'
garb, velvet coat and floppy tie.

Caricature of Oscar Wilde by
'Ape' in *Vanity Fair*. Although
still hankering after a 'notable and
joyous dress for men', Oscar
Wilde finally accepted the
conventional dress of his day and
in the 1890s his clothes were
indistinguishable from those of
any well-dressed man.

Marquis of Hartington

Imp Lemercier & Cie, Paris

Fashion plate, 1875. An example
of the curious custom, which lasted
for a decade or so, of actually
giving names to these tailor's
dummies: in this case the Marquis
of Hartington.

Advertisement in the *Illustrated
London News*, 1890. For the
greater part of costume history it
was the men who wore furs, and
it was not until the 1880s that we
find the first evidence of an
increase in the use of fur in
women's fashions. At the end of
the century men still wore fur
coats but the fur was inside,
showing only in the collar and
cuffs.

AS LIGHT AS A FEATHER

As light as a Feather, advertisement, c. 1890. The bowler, billycock or
'William Coke hat', had been invented in 1850, but at first it was only
worn in the country. By 1890 it had become, in either its rounded or
square shape, quite usual wear in Town.

Count Boni de Castellane driving
in the Bois. Caricature by Sem, *c.*
1900. Count Boni de Castellane
was the supreme French dandy
of the *fin de siècle*. For all *hommes
du monde* (and women of the
monde and the *demi-monde*) it was
obligatory to be seen in public and
a drive in the Bois de Boulogne
served to display not only the
toilette but the *équipage* – both, in
the Count's case, impeccable.

Right A present-day dandy: last
vestige of the neo-Edwardian
revival after the Second World
War.

diversion of a gentleman.' Still less, one might add, of a dandy. Beerbohm then proceeds to give his own ideas of dandyism. 'The dandy,' he says, 'is the "child of his age", and his best work must be produced in accord with the age's natural influence. The true dandy must always love contemporary costume.' This is truly said and disposes at once of Wilde's fancy dress. Beerbohm makes the interesting point that the Army, by inculcating the habit of conformity, 'has given us nearly all our finest dandies, from Alcibiades to Colonel Br*b*z*n *de nos jours*'. And he advises parents who wish their son to be a dandy to send him first into the Army. He adds, maliciously, that 'a sojourn at one of the Public Schools is also to be recommended. The University it were well to avoid.'

Nineteenth-century costume, says Beerbohm, 'as shadowed for us first by Mr Brummell' is quiet, reasonable, 'free from folly or affectation, yet susceptible to exquisite ordering; plastic, austere, economical – ' and *beautiful*. And he goes on to prophesy that it will never change, that the progress of democracy will only strengthen its precepts, which every day are more secure. The rest of this chapter will be devoted largely to showing how wrong he was. But, so long as *la belle époque* lasted, the dandy must have felt quite justified in considering his type immortal.

The supreme French dandy of the period was Count Boniface de Castellane. He was an authentic aristocrat related to the greatest families of the *Ancien Régime*, but, like many of his class, his revenues did not suffice for the scale of expenditure he thought due to his position in Society. He was therefore one of the first to cast his eyes across the Atlantic in search of a sufficiently rich heiress. He found her in Anna Gould, who was extremely plain but whose father had provided her with a dowry of fifteen million dollars.

Back in France, he proceeded to spend it. He built a pink marble palace in the Avenue du Bois with a staircase as grand as that at the Opéra, an immense ballroom and a private theatre with five hundred seats. An orchestra of fifty musicians

'Dancing the Minuet', from *Joie d'Enfants* by M. Mars

welcomed the guests. In addition to this Boni had two châteaux in the country, a house at Deauville, and a yacht.

It goes without saying that his clothes were made by the best tailors and he possessed a prodigious number of suits, including tail-coats of different colours to harmonize with the décor or his mood. It is doubtful if Brummell would have approved of *that*, but in all other respects Boni was the perfect dandy, not least in his *gaspillage*. At length his wife could stand it no longer. Early in January 1906 she left him without warning and divorced him (he had given her plenty of reason) in the following April. The result for Boni was catastrophic. He spent the rest of his life 'in shallows and in miseries', attempting to elude his creditors, acting as an agent for the sale of antiques and writing several books of confessions. With slight variations it is the classical pattern of the dandy's life. Naturally so perfect a dandy had many imitators, and he himself tells us of one, an Argentinian, who copied him in everything. 'If I put on a red tie, on the following day he did the same. If I drove a two-horsed phaeton, he immediately bought one like it. When I became a *député*, he put up for Parliament in his own country. If I made a speech in

the *Chambre* he was present in order to observe my gestures. He was delighted when people told him that he resembled me and his fellow countrymen called him Boni II.' The caricaturist Sem published two identical portraits labelled respectively the 'True' and the 'False'.

It is to Sem indeed that we owe the most convincing portraits of the dandies and *grandes dames* and *grandes cocottes* of the epoch. We can watch them driving in the Bois or supping in some *salle privée*, at Longchamps or Deauville, in all the haunts of pleasure: the aged Leopold, King of the Belgians, the youthful Aga Khan, Cléo de Merode and Liane de Pougy, the whole panorama and phantasmagoria of *la belle époque*.

In his reminiscences Boni de Castellane offers rather malicious thumbnail portraits of the other dandies of his time. There was, for example, his relative the Prince de Sagan, a *gentilhomme* of supreme elegance whose air of a grand seigneur had a hint of the actor about it. Authentic Prince as well as 'prince de la mode', he suggested at once the *Pair de France* and the compère of a revue. His whole attitude, his gestures, his appearance, the black ribbon of his monocle were *chic* in the extreme.

He and Boni de Castellane were much seen together in the days when the former was squandering the Gould millions, and they were jointly responsible for a 'private party' at the Tir aux Pigeons in the Bois de Boulogne which staggered even Paris. There were three thousand guests, two hundred and fifty of whom were invited to an 'intimate' but lavish dinner beforehand. Sixty footmen in scarlet livery were hired to attend the guests and 'group themselves on the grass' in artistic patches of colour. The guests themselves however were protected from 'the discomfort of the evening dew' by fifteen kilometres of carpet. Eighty thousand Venetian lamps were hung in the surrounding trees. The President of the Municipal Council, whom the two dandies went to see to arrange for the hiring of the Tir aux Pigeons, was staggered by the proposals laid before him. He ventured to inquire the object of the projected fête. 'Sir,' said

Caricature by Sem of Boniface de Castellane

the Prince de Sagan, adjusting his eyeglass, 'this fête is given simply for our amusement – simply for our amusement.'

Other great dandies were Count Robert de Fitz-James, 'type de clubman aristocratique', General de Gallifet, and the somewhat mysterious Charles Haas, who was the only Jewish member of the Jockey Club and is supposed to have been the original of Proust's Swann. Count Robert de Montesquiou who figures in Proust as Baron Charles was more an aesthete than a dandy and, as we have noted in the previous chapter, the two things are, to some extent at least, incompatible.

The early years of the twentieth century brought very little change in male attire, except that the stiff white collars were higher than ever. Curiously enough these stiff white collars were worn also with lounge suits and even with Norfolk jackets and knickerbockers. Even women wore them when they were engaged in any kind of 'masculine' activity such as golf. They had indeed become a status symbol, for the Edwardian upper classes were very conscious of the watershed between themselves and 'the great unwashed'. Poor clerks, anxious to keep up appearances, often wore them in celluloid; and those who would not stoop to this expedient wore not only detachable collars (everyone did that) but detachable cuffs and 'dickeys' – detachable shirt fronts with a slit in the middle for a non-operative gold stud.

Lounge suits, however, were increasingly worn, usually with the homburg or trilby hat. The trousers, which were very narrow, had begun to be turned up at the bottom, and the trouser-press, which had been invented in the mid-nineties, made it possible to have a permanent crease, the sharp edge down the front of the trousers. Old-fashioned gentlemen, however, continued, like King George v, to have their trousers pressed with a crease at the side.

Spats were almost universal, although sometimes button boots with cloth tops were substituted. These were replaced about 1910 by shoes, at least among the young and fashionable, and this brought the socks into notice, so that they ceased to be thick and dark-hued and began to be made of lighter materials and in brighter colours. The 'knut' of the period just before 1914 was distinguished above all else by the brightness of his socks. The 'knut', however, was only a kind of suburban dandy at best.

The outbreak of World War I brought *la belle époque* abruptly to a close; and alas! the soldiers who fought in it were deprived even of that dandyism which had been the prerogative of the fighting man from time immemorial. And when the conflict was over it was plain that, like all great social upheavals, it had abolished the most formal of men's clothes. The lounge suit was

Caricature of the would-be dandy from *Punch*, 1900

now universal, the morning coat surviving only for weddings and funerals, Ascot and Lord's.

Would-be dandies did the best they could with the lounge suit with its double-breasted waistcoat and (after 1925) extremely wide trousers. Knickerbockers for golf, and indeed for all country pursuits, became very baggy in imitation of those worn by Guards officers during the war. The Prince of Wales influenced fashion by the introduction of the 'Fair Isle sweater' instead of the waistcoat; and also by wearing a white waistcoat with a dinner jacket. But there was no essential change in male attire between the wars; while with nearly all the men in khaki during World War II and clothes rationing in force, new developments had to wait until the end of the conflict.

The end of World War II saw the emergence of two related but contrasting types, known respectively as the Neo-Edwardians and the Teddy Boys. It is important to distinguish between them. The young Guards officers, returning to civil life, exchanged their military uniform for another kind of uniform. They all still looked exactly alike, wearing clothes which were a direct echo of the masculine modes of the early years of the century. In this there was an undoubted element of nostalgia. Since all clothes mean something, these meant: 'I wish I could go back to an epoch when men *of my class* had all the advantages: "chambers" in Jermyn Street, a man-servant like Jeeves and an income from investments which, if small, was assured.' The bowler hat, purchased in St James's Street, was just a little bit too small; the suit with rather tight trousers and high-buttoned jacket came from one of the bespoke tailors in Savile Row or its immediate neighbourhood. The Neo-Edwardians would have excited no attention if they had strolled down Bond Street on a sunny morning in 1905.

This reaction was quite understandable for men at this social level, but the curious thing is that their styles were echoed, or rather caricatured, by young men who were certainly not of their class: the so-called Teddy Boys. These East End types copied

the Edwardian clothes with a difference. Their trousers were
even narrower, their shoulders much more accentuated and they
wore either a soft felt hat pulled over the eyes or no hat at all.
The general name for them was 'spivs' or 'wide boys'; and the
term 'wide' referred not only to their operations on the black
market but to the actual width of their padded shoulders. The
exaggerated shoulder line was an assertion of masculinity, for
they lived in a world where it paid to be – or at least to be
thought to be – a 'tough guy'. The exaggeration of sexual
characteristic is, of course, typical of female costume, and for
long periods of history of male costume also. One might call
Henry VIII the first of the wide boys. But the whole point of
Brummell's revolution, the whole point of dandyism, is to forgo
this. The clothes of gentility do not say 'I am a man – and
how!' but 'I am a gentleman, and I hope to attract women not
by asserting my masculinity but by demonstrating my member-
ship of a social class.'

Twenty years after the end of the war both Neo-Edwardians
and Teddy Boys were extinct. Both these phenomena were in
the nature of back-eddies. The main line of development showed
once more that male costume evolves by adopting a sports
costume for ordinary wear, and this development was much
aided in the years immediately after the war by the shops selling
'Government Surplus Stores'. The duffle-coat was the Navy's
contribution, the battle-dress the Army's. The motor-cyclist
found in surplus stores a whole collection of useful garments, of
which the sleeveless leather coat is an obvious example, and
flying kit another.

Foreign influences began to threaten the long-accepted
supremacy of English modes. The dashing cut of Italian clothes
and Italian pointed shoes had, for a time, a marked influence on
all but the most conventional. The Americans exploited their
real advantage in what might be called hot-weather clothes for
sport or for ordinary wear and even Englishmen took to the
tropical suit. In London the East End began to challenge the

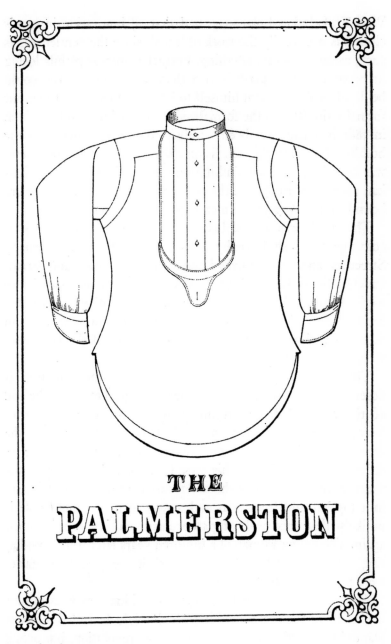

Shirt advertisement, *c.* 1910

8

West End. It has been suggested that all innovation in men's clothes is necessarily the work of 'cads', since the gentleman, as such, cannot innovate anything. Formal attire was plainly losing its prestige. It might still be true than an aspiring banker would be ill-advised to present himself to his superiors in anything but formal attire (that is the formalized version of the clothes which in 1880 it would have been 'caddish' to wear in Town). But the budding film director, television floor-manager, or pop singer was conscious of no such inhibitions and as all three professions had enormous prestige in the post-war years, their clothes were bound to influence young men even of the upper classes.

The result was a duel between Savile Row and what it is convenient to call Carnaby Street. Until the 1960s Carnaby Street was an undistinguished, not to say dingy, short and narrow street in Soho, London's *quartier latin*. It suddenly soared into world fame as the street where young 'with-it' men went for their clothes. And 'with-it' young women, too, for now an astounding thing was happening: the clothes of the two sexes were beginning to overlap and even to coincide.

This phenomenon has not yet received the attention it deserves. What it seems to mean, in sociological terms, is the end of the patriarchal system under which the greater part of (recorded) history has been lived. During all this time the dominant male imposed on women clothes which were as different as possible from his own. One has only to think of the contrast, in the middle of the nineteenth century, between a man in a top-hat and frock coat and a woman in a crinoline. It is unlikely that this peak of patriarchism will ever be reached again. The young women of a hundred years later were repudiating the patriarchal system just as their male contemporaries were repudiating the idea of gentility.

And yet, out of Carnaby Street, something new is even now beginning to emerge, something which might be called the New Dandyism. In effect it accepts the clothes revolution, but uses it to create its own style and chic. New names have arisen to

challenge the prestige of the famous names of Savile Row, and what they are doing is something very similar to what Brummell did at the beginning of the nineteenth century. Perhaps dandyism, which we have tried to understand by studying within strict limits of time and space, is something immortal after all.

Notes on further reading

Honoré de Balzac, *Le Traité de la vie élégante*. Paris.

J. Barbey d'Aurevilly, *Du Dandysme et de Georges Brummell*. Paris, 1861.

Charles Baudelaire, *The Painter of Victorian Life*. Constantin Guys. London, 1930.

Quentin Bell, *On Human Finery*. London, 1947.

Max Beerbohm, 'Dandies and Dandies', in *Works*, London, 1898.

Pearl Binder, *The Peacock's Tail*. London, 1958.

Max von Boehn, *Modes and Manners*. London, 1932.

R. Boutet de Monvel, *Beau Brummell and his Times*. London, 1908.

D. C. Calthrop, *English Dress from Victoria to George V*. London, 1934.

Thomas Carlyle, *Sartor Resartus*. London, 1836.

Count Boniface de Castellane, *Comment j'ai découvert l'Amérique*. Paris, 1925.

A Cavalry Officer, *The Whole Art of Dress*. London, 1830.

W. Connely, *Count d'Orsay, the Dandy of Dandies*. London, 1952.

J. C. Flügel, *The Psychology of Clothes*. London, 1930.

J. C. Flügel, *Man, Morals and Society*. London, 1945.

C. M. Franzero, *Beau Brummell: His Life and Times*. New York, 1958.

E. B. Giles, *History of the Art of Cutting*. London, 1887.

Captain R. H. Gronow, *Reminiscences*, 2nd edition. London, 1842.

Captain R. H. Gronow, *Celebrities of London and Paris*. London, 1865.

Captain R. H. Gronow, *Last Recollections*. London, 1866.

Captain William Jesse, *Life of George Brummell*. London, 1844.

Clare Jerrold, *The Beaux and the Dandies*. London, 1910.

Laurence Langner, *The Importance of wearing Clothes*. New York, 1959.

James Laver, *Taste and Fashion*. London, 1937.

H. Leblanc, *The Art of Tying the Cravat*. London, 1828.

Ellen Moers, *The Dandy*. London, 1960.

Paul H. Nystrom, *The Economics of Fashion*. New York, 1928.

Michael Sadleir, *Bulwer: A Panorama*. London, 1931.

W. Teignmouth Shore, *D'Orsay, or the Complete Dandy*. London, 1911.

W. D. Vincent, *The Cutters' Practical Guide*. London, 1893.

N. Waugh, *The Cut of Men's Clothes*. London, 1964.

Oscar Wilde, *Art and Decoration*. London, 1920.

Acknowledgements

The author and publishers would like to thank the people and institutions below for providing the photographs on the pages mentioned before their names.

70 (*above and below*), 71 (*above and below*), Editions du Chêne (from A. d'Eugny, *Baudelaire, Guys et Nadar*); 99, Ashmolean Museum, Oxford; 104 (*below*), Aquascutum Limited; 29, 43 (*above*), 60 (*above*), 72 (*below*), British Museum; 18 (*above*), Bulletin of Pasadena Art Institute; 57, *Gazette of Fashion*; 67, Librairie Téqui; 60 (*below*), *L'Illustration*; 35, 53, 59, 75, Mary Evans Picture Library; 46, Metropolitan Museum of Art, Harris Brisbane Dick fund; 20 (*below*), Musée du Louvre; 44, National Gallery; 84, 101 (*right*), National Portrait Gallery; 42, *Petit Courrier des Dames*; 20 (*above*), 58, 82 (*left*), 103, Radio Times Hulton Picture Library; 102 (*right*), *Illustrated London News*; 82, *Vanity Fair*; 18 (*below*), 101 (*above and below left and right*), 30, 32 (*above and below*), 38 (*above*), 43 (*below*), 79, 81, 104 (*below*), Victoria and Albert Museum; 101 (*left*), William Gordon Davis.

The pictures on the following pages were taken from the author's collection: 17, 37, 38 (*below*), 39, 40/41 (*above and below*), 83, 102 (*left*).

Index